I0476659

How to
Publish
Your
Book for
Free

Sam Cudney

Other Books by Sam Cudney

Illustrated Tour of Sacred Places in Hawai'i
Hawai'i - A Glimpse into the Past
Welcome to Paradise - Moving to Hawai'i Made
Easy
Cheap Fun in Hawai'i
Declare His Praise in the Islands
49 Things to do on the Big Island
My Name is Not Ernie
True Stories
Historic Churches of New Mexico

Copyright 2015, 2017, 2018, 2019, 2021, 2022
11th edition

This is dedicated to all you aspiring authors. May your dreams come true.

Table of Contents

Acknowledgements	vii
Independent Publishing	1
Getting Started	5
What Makes a Book?	11
Writing Your Book	17
The Publishing Platform Getting Started	25
Formatting for Kindle	31
Format Your Paper Book	39
The Cover	59
Publishing	75
Marketing	87
Details	97
Word Ninja Training	105
Afterword	125

Acknowledgements

I am grateful to my wife for encouraging me, to my dogs for keeping the boogeymen away, to Amazon for providing such excellent independent publishing platforms, and to the Hilton Waikoloa Beach Resort for free wifi and their comfortable mens' spa lounge. I do a lot of work sitting there.

Independent Publishing

Independent publishing is the biggest thing in printing since the invention of moveable type. Anybody with something to say can say it to the world; all you need is access to a computer and the internet. No publisher, no agent, no big investment.

I used to think that writing a book and getting it published was a complex affair, highly competitive and with a large element of luck. I believed that only a select few authors could ever be published and available to the general public.

This is true in the traditional publishing world, but there is another path; independent publishing. In this book I show you how to publish and distribute your book with little or no cost to you. There is no need to spend thousands of dollars for book design, layout, and printing; you can do it all yourself with a few basic tools and some new skills.

I mostly write illustrated books about Hawai'i, aimed at visitors. My wife writes fiction, mostly for young adults. We both produce and market our books worldwide, without upfront costs, from home. You can too.

I use Amazon's independent publishing platform, Kindle Direct Publishing, or KDP. KDP offers both e-book and paperback publishing through the same interface, and has just added an option for hard covers on paper books. There are other platforms such as Barnes and Nobel's NOOK and Apple's iBook for e-books, and Blurb and Lulu for print books, but the Amazon platform is easy to use, free, and has serious marketing muscle so I will focus on it.

This book shows you how to create both a printed version of your book and an e-book. You will —

- earn a bigger royalty,
- get to market instantly,
- retain full artistic control of your work,
- use Amazon's marketing muscle,
- be able to make instant updates,
- have no or little expense,
- and most importantly, get published.

Independent publishing benefits the readers, too. I know that in my genre, the majority of the books on Amazon are independently published. As a result, the reader has a wide variety to choose from at affordable prices. If the other writers and myself were not publishing our own work, prospective readers would have only a few books from which to choose. And, since publishing costs are low (in the case of e-books, practically non-existent), prices are reasonable.

Are there any downsides? Of course, but the benefits may outweigh the disadvantages.

Independently published books do not receive the intensive publicity efforts that the big publishing houses can bring to bear. All publicity is up to you (but there are ways to leverage this). Consequently, the odds against becoming a New York Times best seller are staggering. Then again, if you don't publish at all, the odds are much worse.

You have to do everything. Write the book, illustrate it, design the layout, edit, proofread, edit again, get it into publishable form, shepherd it through the publishing process, promote it, and so on. It's all on your shoulders. You are the author, illustrator, editor, publisher, and promoter.

If you have something to say and are willing to do some work, you can make your book a reality. All you really need is internet access, basic computer skills, and willingness.

I urge you to read this book in its entirety before getting bogged down in details so that you have an understanding of the entire process. While I focus here on publishing through Amazon, the layout and formatting requirements will be essentially the same if not identical for other platforms; the only differences will be in the details of setting up an account and uploading the content and cover.

The publishing process can be complicated and confusing. My intention here is to present a proven process for self-publishing. Where it seems like it will help, I include specific, step-by-step directions. In some instances I suggest multiple approaches and suggest free tools so that you can do as much or little as you want.

You CAN publish your book for free!

Now, let's get started.

Getting Started

So you are going to write a book; or maybe you already have, and are wondering what to do with it. Perhaps it's your first novel, or an analysis of the world economy, or a manifesto for peace, or a collection of your poems, or photo essays on Civil War battlefields. It doesn't matter; it's your book. I can't tell you how to do the writing; the creativity has to come from you. What I can do is show you how to publish it yourself, without spending big money. In fact, it's possible to do the whole process for free.

Before we begin, I want to be clear about costs. The short version is that you can spend as much or as little money as you wish. You can actually publish at no cost whatsoever by using software that you already have and software, templates, and services that are available free, for every step of the writing, formatting, and cover-creation process.

You can also engage professional help for some tasks, or purchase special purpose software. How much you spend and how much work you do is up to you. Unless your book is unusually complex, dependent on unusual formatting, or you simply want to be different, the simple, free approaches can give you a professional-looking result.

It doesn't matter whether you are working on a Mac or a PC; the techniques and even much of the software are the same for both. I will walk you through the process, step by step. Here are the basic steps in publishing your book.

1-Write the Book

While I can't help you much with the content, I can offer some things to keep in mind while you are being creative. While you're writing, think about what the finished book should look like, who it's aimed at, and what you hope to achieve. If possible, you should be thinking about these things before you ever start writing. Do you plan on a paper version, an e-book, or both? I'm assuming both; and why not? There's no significant down side to doing both unless there is some specific reason, such as you are planning a large-print book or a book of large, double-page spreads, or maybe a text or reference with lots of hyperlinks, where doing both will not work well for technical reasons.

For the paper version, think about the finished, or trim, size; that is, the dimensions of the book, such as 6" by 9", or 8" by 12". Think too about how you want the pages to look in terms of line spacing, margins, justification, typeface and size, and how long the book will be. It's never too soon to be thinking about a title and potential cover designs. You can, and probably will, change these things as you go, but it's nice to have an idea about where you are going.

If you are pretty confident about the trim size you'll want for the paper book, you might even start by setting your page size to your finished trim size before you start writing. Like almost everything else, you can change if you want. Later on I'll show you how to get free templates in common printing sizes.

You probably have a preferred word processor. If it's compatible with Microsoft Word and can save or export in .doc or .docx format, stay with it. If not, you will need to change. Really. If you don't already have a Word-compatible word processor, in the next chapter I introduce you to a really good, free alternative to Microsoft Office, Open Office. Apple's Pages also works well and is a not-half-bad layout program in its own right.

There is a reason for abandoning your trusty non-Word-compatible word processor; you will need files in .doc format for your e-book. The Word .doc and .docx file formats are pretty much universally accepted by independent publishing platforms such as Kindle and Barnes and Noble's NOOK, but they can have problems with other file formats.

You will need a .pdf formatted file for the KDP paper book; you might be able to print this out directly if you are using a Mac. Otherwise, there are a number of format conversion programs, both stand-alone and on-line, to create .pdf files from .doc files.

2-Prepare and Format Your Book for Publishing

This is when you make the final decision about trim size for the paper version, and format your book accordingly. You can format your book entirely from scratch, or use a free, pre-designed and formatted template for the paper version.

At this point you will create two versions, an e-book and a paper book, either paper cover, hard cover, or both, so that you can format each for best results in its medium. You will make those final formatting decisions and create the files you need to publish. This is also where you will insert illustrations.

Now is when you will need a moderate level of skill with Microsoft Word to do some things that might possibly be unfamiliar to you. I have added a chapter at the end, Word Ninja Training, with some basic instruction in the necessary Word skills.

3-Create a Cover

The cover and the title are probably the main factors in drawing people to your book. The cover needs to be eye-catching, yet legible and attractive when reduced to near postage stamp-size, as it will be on the pages of Amazon. Again, you can design your own cover, use a professional service, or use free pre-designed templates.

4-Publish Your Book!

Finally, you upload the files to Amazon or whichever platform you prefer, for publishing as a paper book and/or as a Kindle e-book. In this book I describe the processes and how they differ from one another.

For each edition, paper or e-book, you select appropriate categories and key words to help people find it, write a brief description, determine a price, and release it to the world. The publishing process is absolutely free for both. You pay no money; in fact, Amazon sends you money when a copy is sold.

5-Market Your Book

There are many tools you can use; we will touch on a few of the easier ones, including Amazon's free book giveaway promotional program and Vertical Response or Mail Chimp, mailing list management sites that let you send newsletters about your book. This part is up to you.

In the next chapter I will describe book formats, and how paper books differ from e-books.

What Makes a Book?

Or more precisely, what makes an e-book, and what makes a hard copy, or paper, book? Because of differences in the media, the two are not identical. The general content and layout of paper books has evolved over the centuries into a fairly standard format. It's a pretty good idea to stick closely to that format, or risk confusing the reader. E-books, though, are a relatively new phenomenon, with rules shaped by the medium.

A paper book, either soft or hard cover, generally consists of most or all of the following –

Cover. You will need a front cover design, a back cover design, and possibly, depending on the size of your book, a spine design. For the Amazon paper book platform, your final cover layout, front and back, will be a single page encompassing both the front and back covers, in .pdf format, with some other specifics I'll tell you about later. The details are slightly different for soft and hard covers.

Title page. This is a page with the title and author's name. That's it.

Copyright page. This page states that you own the rights to the book. There are many ways to phrase this, but basically, here you assert that you own it and it's wrong to steal. Sometimes authors will add information about their other books, a plea for reviews, or other material here.

Dedication. This is optional, but nice.

Table of contents. You really need this. You can have chapter numbers, or chapter numbers and titles. There are different opinions as to whether fiction should have chapter titles or not. Personally, I think it's a good idea to have chapter titles for fiction, especially if the chapter titles are helpful or interesting.

Acknowledgments. This is where you recognize all those people who helped you along the way.

Blank pages inserted as necessary in this front matter to make some things print on the right-hand page. This is traditional, for some reason.

Introduction. This is where you tell the reader what's going to happen in the book. It can be your first chapter, titled "Introduction," or you can just skip it altogether and jump right in at Chapter 1.

Body of text. Your manuscript. It's helpful as you go along to think about what you want the finished work to look like. By the way, as a general guide, one full page double-spaced Times Roman 12 point text becomes about one full page single spaced text in a book with a trim size (the outer dimensions of the book) of about 5.5" X 8.5," a popular size. This means that if you have 100 pages of text in your manuscript, you'll have a book of about 110 pages printed, including the introduction, table of contents, etc.

End notes, appendices, index, afterword, and other things that go at the end. Chances are that you won't have any, except maybe the afterword. You may not need or want all of these elements, and that's OK. You definitely want the title page, copyright, and table of contents, though.

An e-book such as a Kindle book, on the other hand, has a different layout because of the nature of the medium. Here is a common format that I like; there are no hard and fast rules, but this works.

Cover. You only need the front cover, but it needs to be a specific size, regardless of the trim size of the paper book, and should be uploaded as a .jpg file.

Combined title page and copyright statement.

Dedication, optional.

Table of contents. Ideally, with clickable links to the chapters. I will show you how.

Acknowledgment, also optional.

Introduction.

No blank pages. No need for them.

Body of text. The Kindle format is not kind to illustrations or fancy formatting, or to formatting in general; with limited exceptions, special typefaces and formatting generally goes away, since the Kindle reading software gives the book reader only a very limited choice of typeface. You will notice some examples in this book, if you have the e-book version, of Kindle-specific quirks. Stick with Times Roman or something similar as a typeface, and stay with fairly plain formatting.

End notes, optional index (as clickable links), and appendices.

Why, you might ask, are we combining the title page and copyright for the Kindle version? What happened to the blank pages? When you publish your e-book as a Kindle book, Amazon offers the prospective reader a preview; you've seen these and used them to peek inside the book to see if it's something you want to buy. This preview is limited to about 10% of the actual book. We want the reader to get to the good stuff in our book immediately and not have to pick through blank and almost-blank pages, so rather than waste that valuable space, we jump in as far as we can right away. Trust me; compressing these things won't cause problems, and will get the potential reader involved quicker.

Now let's create a book.

Writing Your Book

We're going to start the process with the body of text, and wrap the other elements around it. If you already have Microsoft Word or (on a Mac) Pages or some other word processor that can export files in .doc format, use what you have. If, however, you are a long-time WordPerfect or WriteNow user, or use anything else that can't export as a .doc or .docx file, it's time to move on. Most publishing platforms favor the near-universal .doc (and usually the related .docx) files. Fortunately, there is a way to get much of the power of Word without spending any money. Let me introduce Open Office. If you already have Word, you can skim through this, but don't skip it.

Open Office is a pretty good free office suite, kind of like Microsoft Office but without some "features." It is basic, but powerful. It is available for both Mac and PC platforms (Linux, too.) Think of it as Office 1993, if there were such a thing, but a little easier to navigate and with very unimaginatively named modules; "Writer," "Calc," "Impress," "Base," and "Draw." You probably can figure out from the name what each one does.

Where do you find Open Office? At the Open Office web site, naturally!

https://www.openoffice.org

Once you've downloaded Open Office and installed it, go ahead and open it up and get to work. If you have already written or started your book with another word processor, you can almost certainly import it into Open Office. Open Office can read a variety of formats including Word Perfect, WinWord, StarWriter, DocBook, Pocket Word, generic .rtf and .txt files, and things I've never heard of. At a minimum, you can probably export your work from your existing word processor as an .rtf or .txt file, but you will lose most of your formatting. Don't worry, you'll get it back when you apply styles. Like Word, Open Office's word processing module, "Writer," features styles, one of the most powerful aspects of any word processor.

I'm not going to attempt to instruct you in all the details of your word processor; there are too many variables, and lots of good on-line tutorials. You will need to be competent with headers and footers, styles, sections, and some of those other little symbols across the top or down the side of the screen. I'll be referring to the chapter on Word Ninja Training in places where you will need these skills.

Styles

The very first thing you should do if you haven't already done so is create at least one custom style for the body of your text. This is absolutely vital. You can find details in Word Ninja Training. Keep it simple to begin with, you can experiment with typefaces, etc. at any time, thanks to the amazing power of styles. Keep in mind that Kindle, like most if not all e-book readers, lets the reader choose type-face and size, so pretty much no matter what you pick it'll probably be read as Times New Roman on a Kindle.

Pick an easy-to-read typeface; single-spaced, or double spaced if it's easier for you to work in, but change it to single space when we get to formatting (the power of styles, again), with either a modest indent at the beginning of each paragraph or, alternatively, a small space (6 points or so) at the end of each paragraph, not both, so the reader can tell where paragraphs begin and end. You can change the any of these details, throughout your manuscript, at any time by modifying the style.

Create another style for your chapter headings; a simple and workable choice is to simply bold the headings and bump up the point size for now, but be sure and make it a unique style used only for chapter headings, because you'll use it later to create a table of contents. Set up styles for any other kind of text format you plan to use; footnotes, sub-heads, bullets, etc. Be consistent in your use of styles, this will pay off later.

That's about it for a novel or collection of fiction or that history of Icelandic volcanoes you've been working on. If you're a poet, or writing an illustrated children's book or something with a strong visual element you will probably prefer to be a lot more creative with the formatting, so have at it. Just remember that the conversion to Kindle format messes with your formatting. What you thought would be Lucida Blackletter with Jazz chapter titles will end up Times

New Roman with Helvetica chapter titles for the Kindle version.

Don't let that stop you, though; you will spin-off a separate Kindle version in the formatting process, so use what you want the final hard copy to have at this step. Remember, you will be making two versions of the same book.

Hint; setting your page size to the dimensions you expect to use for your finished paper book will help you better visualize the appearance of the finished product.

Speaking of Kindle-friendly, embedding graphics and photos can sometimes lead to surprising results, and not the good kind. Size and placement can change for no obvious reason, and two-page spreads just don't work at all. Kindle photo books can be iffy and in general are a bad idea. For one thing, the various readers all seem to treat the book somewhat differently (for example, Kindle books look different on a Kindle, Amazon Fire, iPad, and iPhone, and are small on all readers), not to mention the effects of individual readers' choices for font and size. We'll deal with illustrations later, when we're formatting the book. In the meantime, don't put in things like "picture of kitten here" or use "special" words to indicate where you will add things later. These little Easter eggs have a habit of making it into the finished work. Instead, leave a gap of several lines where you plan to insert something. It's easy to find later when you proofread, which you will do pretty often.

Make things easier for yourself and the reader; insert a page break at the beginning of each new chapter. This is essential for the paper book and makes for a more elegant e-book.

The Kindle conversion also sometimes has problems with footnotes. Sometimes they migrate to the end of the book as a clickable link, or not. Sometimes, the linked footnote doesn't have a return link. Unless they're important, try to avoid them. For best results, keep the formatting simple. At this stage, just write your book. And be sure to proofread rigorously, and have somebody else read it too. By the time you get to this point you won't be able to see errors that others will spot instantly.

Proofreading

This is so important I'm making it a whole section by itself. Proofreading is really a two-step process;

- Spell, grammar, and punctuation check, and
- how does it read?

You will go through these steps multiple times. Don't be discouraged, though; it's worth the effort.

First, run the usual spell and grammar checks with whatever tools your word processor offers. You might add some special words to your dictionary in the process, but be careful with that, it's easy to add misspellings, too.

Then, go back and check for common punctuation problems. Using the "find" function, look for duplicate punctuation such as two periods together, two commas together, a period and a comma together, etc. Then look for two spaces together. This is a no-no. Regardless of what Ms. Grinchwell taught you in 7th grade typing class, it's wrong. It's a legacy of using mono-spaced type like that found on older typewriters, and has been obsolete for quite a long time. Typographic convention has been to use a single space after the period for at least the last couple of centuries. No double spaces after periods!

Once you're satisfied that the spelling and punctuation is good, set it aside for a while; long enough that it'll be at least a bit unfamiliar when you pick it up, a week at the minimum. Then read it again. This is where you'll suddenly realize that you have some re-writing to do. This is a good thing.

This is also a good place to enlist a beta reader; a person who is not familiar with your book and who will read it and give you unbiased feedback about all aspects. Close friends and family do not necessarily make good beta readers because they might not want to hurt your feelings. One way to find a beta reader is to approach your Face-book friends. Ask the beta reader specific questions such as the following.

- What structural changes would make this better/ clearer/more useful?
- What elements or sections do you find boring or unnecessary?
- Is this potentially useful or entertaining to you?

Forgive them for their answers, which might prompt another re-write. Once you're satisfied, set it aside for a while, then go through the proofreading process again. Repeat until you're satisfied that it's the best you can do. At this point you have a manuscript nearly ready to publish.

The Title

You need one. It will probably change as you progress. I suppose it would be interesting to publish a book without a title and perhaps even without an author credit, but why make it harder on your readers? Besides, the publishing platforms we're using absolutely require title and author, so you will have to try that experiment some other time.

Research prospective titles by searching for them to see if they've already been used, and for what? Title duplication might be unavoidable, but you should try. At a minimum, use a subtitle to differentiate your book from others.

The title should say something to attract the reader. It doesn't have to precisely describe the book; *To Kill a Mockingbird* is not a book of instructions for reducing the bird population. On the other hand, *The Dummy's Guide to ...* is pretty clear about its purpose.

Like the cover, the purpose of the title is to attract the reader, so spend some time with it. You might change it a few times.

Summary

- Use a word processor that can create a .doc-format file. If yours can't, switch. Really.

- Use styles for your text, chapter headings, subheads, etc.
- Understand that the Kindle version will probably look somewhat different.
- As you write, leave a gap of a few lines where you plan to insert illustrations, then go back and insert them later. Be sure and re-size them to fit.
- Do put a page break just before each new chapter.
- Proofread! Proofread! Did I mention, proofread?

Common Problems

- Faulty punctuation, including double spaces.
- Duplicating a previously published title.
- Continuity problems; changes in locations, names, etc. that don't make sense in the context of the book. Using two different names for the same character is an example.
- New chapter not starting on new page.

Next, we'll format your Word manuscript for both paper and Kindle. Read both of those chapters, Kindle and paper, even if you only plan on one of these formats because there is quite a bit of useful information applicable to publishing in general spread through the two chapters. You can do it in either order, paper first or Kindle first.

But first, let's get acquainted with the KDP publishing platform. You might need a few of the resources that it brings to you right away.

The Publishing Platform
Getting Started

I like Amazon. They treat the author right. Decent royalties, easy publishing process, very wide distribution, and helpful marketing tools. Chances are, the last time you went looking for a book you went to Amazon; they get literally millions of inquiries a day. Plus, unlike most of the other platforms, you can publish both an e-book and a paper book simultaneously.

As you know, Amazon's e-book platform is Kindle. There is Kindle reader software for just about every electronic device known, except maybe garage door openers and TV remote controls, not to mention the several different varieties of dedicated Kindle readers. The Kindle readers automatically format the book to fit the screen of the reader. Amazon will automatically convert your .doc or .docx file into the appropriate format, either by submitting the .doc or .docx file directly or by converting your file yourself before submittal using Kindle Create, about which more later.

Amazon's KDP also provides a paper publishing platform that accepts your book as a .pdf file and prints paper books with a soft or hard cover, at no cost to you. It is an on-demand process; books are printed digitally when they are ordered. The books are bound with what is known as a "perfect" binding, in which the inside 0.125" or so of all the pages are glued together, then the cover is wrapped around the book and glued along the spine and the left-hand margin. This is a durable binding, much nicer than the usual fall-apart paperback binding.

The two platforms, Kindle and KDP paper, are linked; you can publish both the Kindle edition and the paper edition simultaneously, using the same description, key words, etc. and they will display together in Amazon's vast online catalogue. By making them appear together, on the same page in the Amazon book listings, reviews are automatically combined, and it is reviews that sell books on Amazon.

The other main e-book platforms such as iBooks and NOOK, have less-helpful interfaces, don't have as broad distribution, and may not have a paper publishing platform. Other paper publishing platforms such as Blurb do not have Amazon's incredible reach or no-cost-to-the-author printing. Why not stick with the 800-pound gorilla of publishing?

To get started, you are going to need to set up an account for KDP. You can, of course, use your existing Amazon account, but if you set up a new account in the name of, for example, *mynameauthor@gmail.com,* you can enlist outside help without opening up your Amazon account to strangers. Besides, you will want a separate email address for your fans to communicate with you, so why not start now?

Setting up the account is free, and if you provide a routing number and account number, Amazon will make royalty payments directly to your bank. Otherwise, they will mail you a check.

Amazon will also want the basic information necessary for Federal 1099 forms to report royalty payments. The IRS requires Amazon to report your royalties for tax purposes. Receiving a 1099 for royalty payments is probably the only time getting tax-related documents is something to look forward to. Once your account is set up, you're ready to start the publishing process. You can take some of the necessary steps even before your book is finished.

It will help to read through this chapter before starting, though, so you have an idea about what's coming up. Some things won't make sense at first, until you actually get to the act of publishing. Nothing will get published accidentally until you actually request it, so you can't really do any harm.

Start by logging in to your KDP account and going to your Member Dashboard. This is where all your books will be displayed, along with their status and any messages from Amazon. Click on either the new Kindle or new paper book button. It will take you to the introductory pages. This is a good time to explore the whole site, looking at all of the pages.

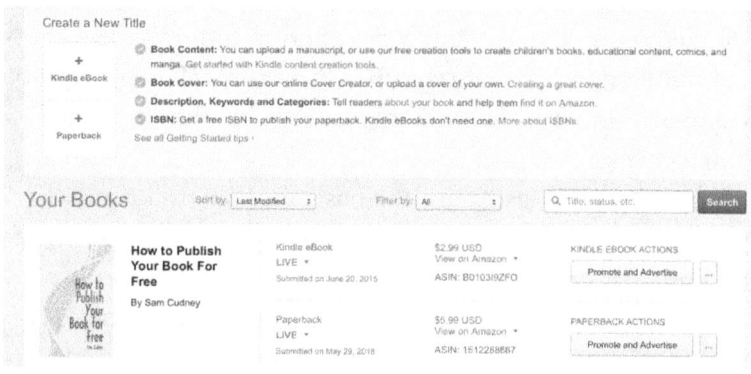

You can enter a name for your project; the book title is an obvious choice. Or not; this is an exploratory trip, just click through the pages to get familiar with the platform until you're ready to commit to a title. Most things can be changed later.

You can enter the parts you know at this point; the book title if it's different from the project name, your name as author, any contributors (chances are there aren't any), and your expected publication date.

You will find a place in the paper book section where Amazon asks for an ISBN and offers to assign one for free. The ISBN, or International Standard Book Number, is a permanent identifier of your book. The number assigned by Amazon is tied to that edition; you can't transfer this book with this ISBN to another publisher once it's published on Amazon, but you can transfer the book to another platform with a new ISBN. I'm assuming that at this point you want the simplest, least-expensive possible publishing process. Once assigned to a book, the ISBN cannot be changed, but you can still change most of the details. For more about ISBN, go to the chapter on Details.

You can pick your interior print mode for the paper book—color or black and white—and choose the paper color. If there is any color in the book, the whole book is a color print job, and white paper is the better choice. If there's no color, either paper, off-white or white, is fine but black and white illustrations work better with white paper.

Amazon's KDP platform lets you upload the Kindle file and the paper file separately; you can do either or both, and you can do them in either order. I prefer doing the Kindle version first, since it can be easily done with the edited Word file or better yet, the Kindle Create file, before I finish formatting for the paper version. You can do it either way, though.

You can download formatted templates for your paper edition directly from the KDP paper book section, or just search "KDP templates." More on this later. If you haven't already thought about the physical size, or trim size, of your book, now is a good time. If you're not sure, experiment with sizes that seem reasonable to you so that you can "test fit" the book into multiple trim size templates to see which you like. The templates are free, in Word format, and relatively easy to use, although they do require some skill with Word. The chapter on Word Ninja Training has lots of details on this.

You should also download Kindle Create from the KDP site. Kindle Create is a program offered by Amazon that converts your Word.doc file into Kindle's native format and gives you a chance to see how it will appear on various Kindle readers. It also can create a hyperlinked table of contents (meaning, clicking on the chapter title in the table of contents takes the reader to that chapter) and do some light-duty formatting. I strongly recommend using it.

Speaking of Kindle Create, Version 1.44.13 and later offer the option of creating both the paper and Kindle version automatically, at the same time, from your .doc manuscript. This is nice, but the formatting controls are limited, particularly for the paper version. I'm assuming here that you are willing to do a little extra work in exchange for more control over the look of the finished product. Even if you choose to let Kindle Create generate your final paper version, you will still need to do quite a bit of formatting and design; Kindle Create is one more tool to help you along.

Now that you have explored the publishing platform, let's start making your Kindle book.

Formatting for Kindle

Kindle (and NOOK and iBook) e-books have slightly different formatting requirements from the paper version. You can start with either one, paper or Kindle, and make the changes to accommodate the formatting requirements of the other version later. Because something has to be first, I'm assuming here that you will start with the Kindle version, but it's not absolutely necessary to do it this way.

Basically, you begin with your Word manuscript, and make a few style changes and add the additional Kindle-specific front matter and illustrations. You then have the option of processing the file through Kindle Create, which I recommend, or uploading the .doc or .docx file directly to KDP, which will manage the conversion more or less automatically. Similarly, Barnes and Noble's NOOK platform, which uses the common EPUB format, also accepts books in .doc format and does the conversion automatically.

Kindle books use a format for e-books that allows limited use of illustrations as well as some flexibility in text, although illustrations and non-standard typefaces can sometimes have unexpected results. You might be surprised when you review the converted book, so be prepared to make some changes. You will later take that same manuscript, add the front matter pages, and format it for the paper version. **Hint; set the size of your illustrations to be a bit smaller than the size of the manuscript page and they will display full-width on the reader, rather than as a tiny little picture embedded in the text.** Here's how you create the Kindle document. First, modify each of the styles you used so they are single-spaced if they are not already. Just select each style by clicking on its far right edge in the palate (in Word), then select "Modify Style" from the drop down. Once that opens, select Format in the lower left corner and change your spacing from double to single spaced.

Insert the Front Matter

Make a title page. Insert a page break before the beginning of your text to add a new page. Type your title about 1/3 of the way down from the top on this new page, in a large typeface. If you can, match the typeface and layout you plan to use for the cover. Near the bottom of that page, type your name. Center both, or align to one side or the other, whatever looks good to you.

Next, make a page break just after your name and type in your copyright, if you have not already created a copyright page. It can be as simple as "Copyright 2021 {*my name*} all rights reserved." Your foreword, if you have one, can go here as well.

A dedication is optional; if you have someone to thank, do it, or skip it altogether. Either way, insert a page break ahead of the dedication page if you have one.

Make a table of contents. Kindle Create can make a hyperlinked table of contents, which is a good reason to use it, but you will need something to start with. You will need one anyway for the paper version, and it's pretty easy to create in Word. Details are in the chapter on Word Ninja Training. It will save you time later.

Make sure your illustrations, etc. are where and how you want them.

Run spell check again, just because.

Why are we single-spacing? The usual printing convention is to have spacing between the lines, called "leading," about the same nominal height as the typeface plus 20%; that is, if you use 12 point type, the leading will be about 14.4 points. You can get this spacing in Word for your paper version, the chapter on Word Ninja Training shows how, but for now we'll leave it single spaced. Kindle Create will do what it wants to do anyway, so spacing doesn't matter that much for e-books and single spaced text looks more like how it will look on the e-book reader.

Kindle does not play well with exotic typefaces, so you might find your choice of Comic Sans and Baskerville Old Style changes to Arial and Times in the Kindle edition.

It bears repeating that Kindle can also do violence to tricky formatting, images, and pretty much anything that isn't straight up text; if you're reading this as a Kindle book you've already noticed this.

There should be a page break after the title page, and a page break before and after the table of contents page. Those should be the only page breaks in the front matter. You will have page breaks at the beginning of each chapter of the book.

Double-check your illustrations, if any. Once again, you should insert your illustrations already re-sized to a bit less than the width of your manuscript page less the margins. If you've created the manuscript in, for example, a 6" wide template, set the width of illustrations at about 4.5." Sometimes KDP has problems with illustrations, and this will help.

Save this file with a unique name that indicates that it is the final formatted Kindle file. You can, or should, run spell check again. It will amaze you how many errors you will still find.

Either way, you should end up with a .doc file with no blank pages. That file contains your entire, complete Kindle manuscript.

Final Kindle Formatting

If for some unfathomable reason you are not using Kindle Create, you could be ready to publish at this point. You can just upload your .doc file and be done, but you would be wise to take advantage of Kindle Create; it helps to make the translation process much smoother. You can upload a .doc file directly to KDP, but it will not have a working table of contents. For that alone, Kindle Create is worthwhile. Kindle Create takes your manuscript .doc file and turns it in to an e-book in Kindle's native format, ready to go, and lets you see how it will look in the common Kindle reader sizes. It's not quite perfect, but it'll save lots of time and effort. The final result is a file in .kpf format; that's the one that you will upload.

Kindle Create will also take your chapter headings and Word-created table of contents (you did use a separate, unique style for chapter headings, didn't you?) and create a Kindle table of contents for you. If you didn't make a table of contents or list of chapter titles in Word, Kindle Create will attempt to identify chapter titles and let you choose which are in the table of contents.

You now have a book formatted for uploading to KDP for publishing as a Kindle book. Congratulations! We'll deal with the actual upload and publishing later.

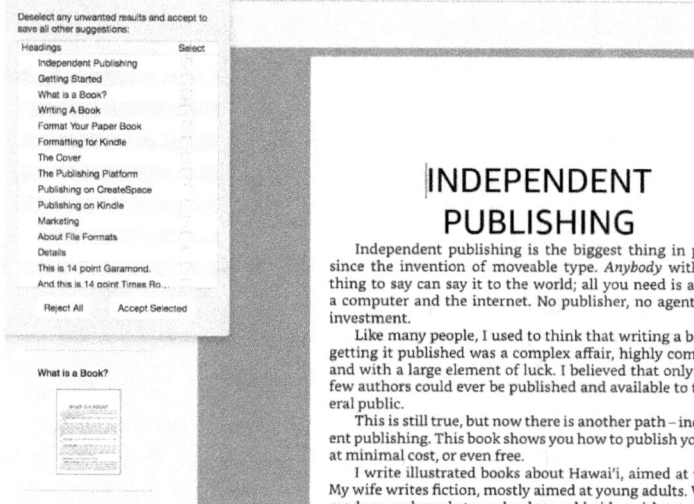

A really nice feature of Kindle Create is preview; it shows you how your book will look on a variety of readers. This is your opportunity to review it one more time, making sure you have the correct version of the book, and that page breaks are in the right places, and that the illustrations look good. A page break before each chapter is important, it makes it much more readable. All of the chapter titles or numbers should be in the table of contents, and there should be no glaring errors such as big blank spaces or hidden characters suddenly appearing, etc. Pay special attention to the common problems below.

Summary

- You can use Kindle Create on your Word manuscript

to format and create the table of contents, and create a .kpf file.
- Save the Kindle file with the minimum of formatting.
- You can upload either a .doc file or the Kindle file, kpf, (which probably stands for Kindle Publishing File) to Kindle. Kindle Create can make things easy.

Common Problems

- Wrong format, such as .pdf for Kindle.
- Extra blank pages or awkward page breaks in Kindle version.

Format Your Paper Book

Formatting for other paper platforms such as Blurb and Lulu will be very similar to formatting for KDP but the details will differ. I'm going to stick with KDP here.

If you are doing only a paper book, either soft or hard cover (the book internals are pretty much the same, just the cover is different) you might have been tempted to skip the Kindle discussion, but resist that urge. And even if you are only planning an e-book, you should look through this chapter anyway to see what a paper book involves. You might change your mind later, although you won't need to actually do all of the formatting described in this chapter if you are doing Kindle-only. It's a good idea to read about the details anyway because I refer to them in other places.

There is no "correct" order for creating the two versions; you can create the paper version first, format it and use that as the basis of the Kindle edition, or the other way around. Just read both the paper book and e-book chapters and decide what you are going to do. Either way, formatting for the paper book and the e-book are sufficiently different that you create two similar but not identical versions. The Kindle version is based on a the completed, ready-to-go manuscript with minor changes, while the paper version is more complex. The manuscript is the same.

Important; regardless of whether you start with the e-book or the paper book, keep in mind that each platform – Kindle, Kindle paper – needs your book in the correct format. Kindle needs either a .doc or a .kpf file for the e-book. The Kindle paper publishing platform needs a .pdf. This is very important.

Since you're reading this book, it's pretty unlikely that you would be using a full-fledged layout program such as InDesign or QuarkXpress. Unless your book relies on double page bleeds or text wrapped in a spiral or has other unusual elements, chances are good that you can do the job in Word or Pages.

Kindle Create can also make a paper version of your book at the same time that it makes the Kindle e-book version. However, the formatting tools in Kindle Create are very limited and awkward, and the resulting book will lack the finished polish of the version you can make in Word. For that reason I am sticking with Word to format the paper version, and Kindle Create to just convert the e-book version into a Kindle-readable form.

You have two main options for formatting the paper book.

Option 1 - Pre-made Template

Use one of KDP's templates. This is a good bet for first-time authors. This approach has the advantage of having the margins, etc. set. It may require learning some new Word skills, as you will have to customize the template. You will need to be familiar with Sections, Headers and Footers, Page Numbers, and a few other Word features. The chapter on Word Ninja Training will help you through. If you do it this way, it's a good idea to actually write your manuscript in the template, or copy and paste it, if you have it already written, so you can see how it will look as a book. You can experiment with trim sizes with a little copy and paste, too. And speaking of trim sizes, hard cover books have fewer trim sizes available, so pick your final trim size accordingly.

Option 2 - From Scratch

Pretty much what it sounds like; define all the elements of a book yourself, starting with a blank page. If you're reasonably proficient in Word, this should be fairly easy. If you aren't very proficient in Word, the chapter on Word Ninja Training will be a valuable resource.

Here are more details about each option.

Using a Pre-made Template

The templates give you a starting point, with margins and trim size and front matter already roughed-out, and are a good choice for beginning publishers. You can easily modify the margins, front matter, etc. The defaults are reasonable and will result in a good-looking book. The biggest down side is that you will still need to exercise your Word skills to fine tune the template. Word Ninja Training to the rescue!

To download the templates, either set up your KDP account as I described in the chapter on The Publishing Platform and download the templates from within your account, or go directly to this web site;

https://kdp.amazon.com/en_US/help/topic/G201834230

If you have a manuscript ready, you can just copy and paste it into the template and have a ready-to-print book.

Just kidding. It's not quite that easy. Almost, though.

As of this writing, Amazon has two choices for the templates. You can download either a set of "blank" templates, or templates with sample content. The blank templates are just a single page of the appropriate dimensions, with margins set at a reasonable default; pretty simple, and not a lot of help. The templates with sample content include "dummy" front matter and have chapter section breaks. I am going to refer to the templates with content in this book because they provide a good starting point.

When you download the templates, either blank or with content, you get a group of ZIP files labeled with several languages; English, German, etc. Save the one(s) that you want and discard the rest. When you unzip the file in your chosen language(s), such as English, you will find (in the case of English) 16 separate Word documents in common printing page sizes.

The "blank" ones are just that; blank except for a sentence saying to start your text there. The pre-made templates with content, however, are actually pretty complex.

They have the common front matter elements—title page, dedication, contents, acknowledgments—as well as blank pages where needed, and headers, footers, and page numbers. They look good. They can be clumsy to use as-received, though, unless you understand how to create and manipulate page- and section breaks, headers, and footers.

But there is hope! It's really not that hard, just something that lots of otherwise-skilled Word users are not used to. The chapter on Word Ninja Training explains more.

Basically, the issue is that the templates use a new section for almost each page of the front matter, and a new section for each chapter. This is overkill for most projects.

"Sections" are a powerful Word tool that allows you to re-start almost all of the document characteristics. You can change margins, page size, number of columns and, most applicable here, headers and footers, in a new section, while retaining styles and other features.

The section breaks in the templates are so the front matter is paginated where appropriate with Roman numeral page numbers, to accommodate changing headers and footers, and a lot of other features that you may or may not want. You can customize the template to suit your specific needs, deleting things you don't want. We'll get to it in a little bit.

You can see the section breaks by using the "reveal formatting" option, either in the "View" tab or by clicking on the paragraph symbol, the thing that looks like a backwards letter "P," in the ribbon bar. Section breaks are parallel horizontal lines that say "section break" in the middle. Page breaks are parallel horizontal lines that don't have any text.

You can either fill in the information in the front matter sections as appropriate and then copy and paste your manuscript a chapter at a time, adding page and section breaks as needed and re-creating headers and footers and re-starting page numbers as needed; or modify the template to simplify things a lot. I favor the latter, simpler approach, but let's talk about the all-out version first; especially the part about headers and footers and page numbers.

In Word, a header or footer stays the same in a section. Period. To change the header or footer, you need a new section. Since the template uses a new section for each chapter, and you might even add sections with blank pages for the blank page before a right-hand chapter beginning, you will have to copy and paste the header and/or footer into each section, or use the "Same as Previous" link. Word Ninja Training has more details on this. It's quite a bit of work, but results in a very nice, professional job.

Likewise, if you insert blank pages as sections, you will definitely have to copy and paste headers and footers, and re-start page numbers. If chapter 1 ended on page 17, you need a blank where page 18 would be, and chapter 2 to start on page 19. You can do this in Word.

If your Word skills are up to the challenge, this is the way to go. If you don't feel comfortable with it, there is an alternative; not quite as elegant, but workable. If you are not confident in your skills, the alternative will still give you a good looking book with a simplified layout. Unless a reader is looking for minute details of layout, no one will ever know.

The Alternative

Download the KDP template with content, and start cutting. Basically, you want to delete everything after the first chapter of the template — section breaks, page breaks, and text — so you have only one section after the front matter. Trust me; it will be fine. The headers will not change from chapter to chapter, and you can might even skip the "start each section of the text on a right-hand-page" thing if you don't want to insert blank pages, which is a departure from normal publishing practice, but will look OK.

You now have a new, simplified and slightly more casual template, with place markers for the front matter plus a section just for your manuscript, and no blank pages between chapters. You can paste your manuscript, without the front matter you added for the Kindle version, into that last section of the template, and fill in or delete the individual parts of the front matter as appropriate.

A word about starting chapters on the right-hand side (called the *recto* by printers. The left-hand page is called the *verso*. Left and right together are a *spread*.) This is a very old printing convention, and is rigorously observed in academic and technical publications, among others. I am sticking with it here for the most part because it is good practice, but as with most things, feel free to ignore or change it; it is your book. The alternative proposed above will probably result in some chapters starting on the left side instead of the right, which is a departure from common practice, but I suspect most readers will not notice or care.

Layout From Scratch

If you want to go it alone, you can create your layout from a blank page, setting page size, margins, headers, footers, page and section breaks as you see fit. It's not a lot more work than starting with a template, and there is less fiddling around with deleting section breaks. It does require a bit more boldness, since you are starting with nothing.

However you decide to do it, there are basic design elements common to almost all books.

Margins

For a trim size of 5.5" X 8.5" like this book, set the left and right margins between 0.75" and 1." The pre-formatted template sets the margins at 0.76" for this trim size, which I think is a little small. For large books of more than about 100 pages, if your word processor allows it (Word does; it's under Format:Document in the tool bar), set the inside margin, or gutter, slightly larger by about 0.125." We can come back and adjust as necessary once we see the total page count and have some idea of what kind of extra margin we need on the inside.

This might not be obvious, but when the book is bound, the inside edge, closest to the binding, will lose a little visible margin due to the binding, so you want to be sure that the inside margin is wide enough that text doesn't get lost. It becomes more of an issue with thicker books because they resist being folded open more than smaller books, so more text will be hidden near the fold.

For bigger trim sizes, set the margins a little wider, so the margins are each between 10% to 20% of the trim width. This is not a hard and fast rule, just a guide that gives an attractive margin for most books. The margin might be an important element in your book design, or you might want to leave space for the reader to make notes, in which case you make the margins whatever you think is right.

Set the top and bottom margins large enough to accommodate headers and footers. A top margin of up to about 1.2 times the side margin is generally attractive, so if the side margin is 0.75," set the top between 0.75" and 1." Again, this is a general guide. The pre-formatted template sets a top margin of 0.76," but for this book I increased the top margin to 1" because I thought it looked better.

At the bottom, set the margin at least as big as the top margin, but no more than about 1.5 times the top margin. This is only a general guide to a starting point. Place your page numbers and a page header (the book title is a good choice for a header) and adjust their spacing and the top and bottom margins until you have an attractive page. Either center the page number, or put it at the extreme outside edge, aligned with the edge of the text, either at the top or bottom of the page. Make it look good to you. Bigger margins can give more of a "frame" effect to the text, while smaller ones can make the text look more serious and scholarly. Big margins also give the reader a place to make notes, which is sometimes helpful in non-fiction.

Page Numbers

Usually, the front matter pages are numbered in lower case Roman numerals; ii, iii, iv, etc. It's really up to you. The first page of your text will be page 1, and there should not be any page numbers on the preceding blank page. It's also a common convention to not have the page number or header appear on the first page of the text. This is another option in Word. Word Ninja Training will show you more.

Now, you are seeing your book as a book. Look at the "picture" of the page; the margins, the typeface and size, all the things that go into the look of the book. Print out a page or two and cut it down to your printed size so you can have a better idea about what it's like to hold the finished product. How does it look to you? This is a good time to make adjustments. Changes will get much more complicated later on.

Illustrations

If you have relatively simple illustrations or other non-text things, fit them in after the text is written and inserted in to the template. Remember to re-size them before inserting them. You left some gaps to mark the spots, right? Do not use a "secret" word to mark illustration locations; they have a habit of finding their way into the finished work. In Word, just drag your .jpg or .png file into the text where you want it. Keep the picture width at about the column width, or a little less. Really big pictures can cause problems, as can complex graphics, by running into places they aren't supposed to be in.

Hint; "Clear Formatting" in the Word Styles palette for your illustrations, unless you really want them to have the same format as the text.

Make sure your illustrations are high resolution; 300 dpi (dots per inch) or so, or they'll look awful. A lot of clip art and free illustrations available on the internet are in a very low resolution, 72 dpi format, and will look just terrible when printed. You can check by printing them, or just opening them in Mac's Preview software, or Paint on a PC, which will tell you the resolution. If you want color illustrations, your printing cost for the paper version will soar compared to black and white, but color makes no difference in cost for the Kindle edition. On the other hand, some Kindle readers display in black and white only, so color might be wasted. In general, unless color adds significant value, stick with black and white.

If you are using color and have the skills, you should use a tiny bit less color saturation for color illustrations than you otherwise would, and make all the illustrations a little lighter than you think they ought to be. This is because the digital printing process tends to make things darker and muddier. This is true for black and white as well; make the illustrations lighter than you think they should be and they'll look much better. You will see the results when you proof the book, and can go back and correct things, but start with a lighter, less-saturated illustration. Digital printing sometimes "muddies" illustrations.

Suppose it's something where the illustrations are vital, such as a children's book, or a book on art? Same thing; high resolution, a bit less saturation, and a bit lighter than normal. Again, start with illustrations re-sized to fit the page before you place them.

What if you have illustrations or graphics in other formats? Word can support most of the common formats, but Kindle can only manage .jpg, .gif, .png, and .bmp, so make sure all your graphics are in one of these formats. You might have to do some conversion from one format to another. Mac's Preview software does some format conversions, as do a number of on-line sites. Chances are, though, that if you're using a photo, it's a .jpg, and if you're using a drawing, it's a .bmp or .pd, so you're OK.

While we're on the subject, don't use any material without permission, unless it's specifically made available for use! It's tempting to search the Internet for just the right photo or drawing, download it and use it. Don't do that, unless it's specifically identified as free, or you comply with the terms of the copyright. Some images are copyrighted but are available for free use. Read the fine print to be sure.

You might want to use drawings or do some photo editing for illustrations or for your cover. If your usual photo editing software isn't up to the job, you can download two excellent free Mac programs for photo editing and drawing, GIMP and Inkscape. GIMP is a multi-platform photo-editing program similar to PhotoShop. It is complex, runs slowly, but is extremely powerful. Inkscape is a vector drawing program similar to Adobe's Illustrator, but more user-hostile.

For PC's there're also PhotoPad and Picassa for photo editing, and Affinity's very powerful DrawPlus Starter Edition for drawing.

Both GIMP and Inkscape have on-line tutorials and YouTube demonstrations, as do PhotoPad, Picassa, and DrawPlus. You will be learning a fairly complicated bit of software, so plan on spending some time and effort. All of these tools are complex and powerful and get the job done.

Just be sure your illustrations are in .jpg, .png, .gif, or .bmp format; anything else can cause problems with the conversion process.

Completed Book Format

Now let's finish the book design. We described a common book format earlier, but here it is again, in step-by-step detail. Set up your book like this and you have the starting point for both the paper and Kindle versions. You can easily make changes to the paper version for the Kindle version, if you're doing the paper version first, or add elements to the Kindle version to create the paper version. Hard cover and soft cover versions will have the same format.

First comes the front matter; the title page, copyright, etc. Traditional paper book publishing can have many specialized pages in the front matter; we simplify it here. If you are starting with a pre-defined template, you will already have these elements. Delete or leave out the parts you aren't using. I am assuming here that you are starting with a template.

The order of the pages in the front matter is usually as follows—

- Title page
- Copyright Page
- Dedication
- Blank page, if you have a Dedication
- Table of contents
- Blank page
- Acknowledgements (if you have them)
- Blank page, if you have Acknowledgements
- Introduction or first page of book

The important thing here is that the Title page, the Dedication, the Table of contents, the Acknowledgements, and the Introduction or first page all be on the right-hand page of the finished layout for the paper book. That is why we stick in blank pages. Some of these elements will be combined in the Kindle version, but for the paper version, you need them on separate pages. The template includes blank pages for the front matter.

Title Page

Type your title about 1/3 of the way down from the top, in a large typeface. Match the typeface and layout you plan to use for the cover. Near the bottom of that page, put your name. Your name or pen name must appear inside the book, and it must match the name you use when you upload the book to Kindle Direct Publishing. Try and make it look sort-of like the outside cover.

Copyright Page

On the copyright page, type in your copyright towards the bottom of the page. It can be as simple as "Copyright 2021 {my name} all rights reserved," or it can be a complex exposition on copyright, complete with dire threats that are pretty much unenforceable. You can also stick in disclaimers explaining that all the characters are fictional, etc. as appropriate. It doesn't matter how much detail you include; you have copyright as soon as you write the manuscript, and no amount of threats will dissuade a dedicated plagiarizer. Just state the facts; you own the book and it's wrong to steal.

This is also a place where some authors mention their other books and their web site, and suggest to readers that a review on Amazon would be welcome. You can also put the suggestion of a review at the very end of the book as an afterword; or better yet, do both.

Dedication

If you include a dedication, it should on a right hand page of the printed book with an even number of pages before it. You might have to add a blank page, but most likely if you are following this layout, the copyright page will face the dedication.

Table of Contents

You can create your table of contents directly in Word after you're done formatting the text. Just start it on a right-hand page of the printed book by making sure there are an even number of pages ahead of it; you might have to insert a blank page before it. The chapter on Word Ninja Training has detailed instructions. Do this last, after you are completely done writing the book.

Acknowledgment

This is also optional, and comes after the table of contents and before the introduction or first chapter. Once again, it must be on the right-hand side of the layout, so make sure there are an even number of pages before it. We will keep going back to that even number of pages rule. If you are using either version of the pre-formatted template, you already have separate sections for these elements.

Manuscript; the Body of Text

Paste your manuscript into the template, either a chapter at a time into each section if you are using the full-out, downloaded template, or the whole manuscript at once if you are using the alternative, simplified version. You do not need to copy the front matter from the Kindle layout, if you've done that already; just the text.

Set your line spacing–leading is the printer's term– as described in Word Ninja Training to something between 10% and 30% of the typeface size for your book text style. This is a common printing convention. Double spaced looks awkward, and single spaced is a bit tight for easy reading. You might want to adjust the leading for all of your styles to something that looks good to you.

Next, set up your header, footer, and page numbers. Be sure the first page of the book body has no header, footer, or page number. Word Ninja Training shows you how. If you are using the simplified version of the template, you will have page numbers and headers and footers on all the following pages, beginning with "2" on the second page.

Make sure each chapter starts on a new, odd-numbered page, on the right-hand side. You may need to add page- or section breaks, depending on whether you are using the as-downloaded template or the simplified version, to have your chapters begin on the right.

This is where you catch those widow and orphan lines, strange page breaks, and other problems. Fix everything before you make the table of contents. The table of contents will be your last step.

A word about widows and orphans; Word simply lacks the sophisticated tools to do a great job of controlling spacing between letters, which is necessary to eliminate widows and orphans. If your only choices are to either have a blank line at the page bottom or start a new paragraph with a single line at the bottom, either will work, but never start a page with less than a full line of text (two or more is better) at the top. It looks terrible.

Afterword

You can also insert an afterword right after the end of your book where you thank the readers, strongly suggest that a review on Amazon would be welcome, announce your next book, or whatever seems appropriate to you. Thanking the reader is always nice. If you choose to do this, you can start a new section after your manuscript, delete the header and footer, and put another page break at the beginning of the afterword. Or, just carry on through as part of the previous text. Don't forget to put a blank page if necessary just before the afterword so there is an even number of pages ahead of it. These blank pages are important in the paper version.

And now, you can make your table of contents.

Final Formatting for Paper Publishing

At this point you are pretty much done with the formatting for the paper version. Changes and revisions are still possible at this point, but be sure and go back and check the table of contents page numbers if you make any changes, as even small changes can throw off the page numbers. Changes in margins will dramatically affect the layout. You may be able to make changes such as re-phrasing or adjusting breaks and/or spacing to eliminate widow or orphan lines. Try to have the text on pages that will face one another end at the same place on the bottom of the page.

If there are any adjustments to be made, make them now. Look at the page; is the line spacing good? Do the margins work with the "picture" of the page? Do you still like your typeface choices? These things matter to the paper version. This is a good time to go back and check illustration placements and sizes. Word sometimes is not kind to illustrations.

All that remains for the paper version is more proofreading, and maybe inserting blank pages if needed before the dedication, table of contents, acknowledgments, and/or first page of text so that there are an even number of pages ahead of each; and finally, converting the file to a .pdf.

Read this part carefully; each of these pages–dedication, table of contents, acknowledgements, appendices, index, and first page of text–should have an even number of pages ahead of them in the paper edition so that these pages appear on the right-hand side of the published paper book. This didn't matter for the Kindle edition, where we don't want blank pages, but this is the convention for hard copy books, for no particular reason other than it's always done that way. It's more professional looking to follow the conventions.

Now you have a book; all the front and back matter, the body of the text, everything is exactly as it's going to appear in the printed book. The very last step is to save it as a .pdf, either by printing it as a .pdf if you have a Mac, or using an on-line format converter.

But wait! There's more! This a good time to review your book again. The .pdf file will be the closest thing to how your book will actually print, so you will get a good idea of the page "picture," margins, pagination, etc. If you are satisfied with the look of the book, print your pdf and move on to the cover.

Summary

- Save yourself a lot of work by using a pre-formatted template in the trim size of your choice.
- Include the relevant parts of the front matter; title page, acknowledgements, dedication, table of contents, etc. as applicable. Start each element, and the book text, on a right-side page.
- Save the final KDP paper book file in ready-to-publish form, with front matter, etc. as a .pdf file.

Common Problems

- Wrong format, such as .pdf for Kindle or .doc for KDP paper.
- Dedication, foreword, table of contents, introduction not on right-side page for paper version.
- Page numbers on front matter material.
- Paper version not formatted for trim size.
- Widow and orphan lines.

The Cover

You need one of these, too. The cover is what sets your book apart from the rest; it's the literary version of curb appeal. It should make a statement to draw the reader in. You will use versions of the same cover for both paper book — hardback or soft — and e-book.

Look at covers on the paperback rack in any store; rippling muscles and brawny six-pack abs on the bodice-ripper romances, explosions and rockets and flying bullets on the action adventures, blood and bodies on the mysteries, and tedious, boring covers on the books you're not interested in. The cover is the summary, the trailer, the "buy me." It needs to be interesting, attractive, and tell something about the book.

You might find creating a cover to be harder than writing the book. Fortunately, KDP, both the Kindle platform and the paper platform(s), can create a cover for you and will let you change the cover at any time, even after the book is published. The cover can be difficult for two big reasons;

You have to imagine a cover design. This might be challenging.

It can be a lot of work. You have to do the design, using possibly unfamiliar tools, while satisfying a fairly rigorous and unyielding set of requirements for the layout. More on this later.

There are three options for creating a cover.

Option 1 - Easiest – You can have Kindle Direct Publishing create covers for you, using their excellent on-line cover creation tools. This is the simplest approach and is good for first-time authors. It's also free. The cover will be serviceable and you can customize it to some extent.

Option 2 - Most Flexible – You can create your own cover using your own software, and upload it. This is flexible, but might be complex. You can also buy an inexpensive pre-designed cover and either format it for your book, or work with the designer to format it.

Option 3 - Professional Cover – You can hire a professional or enlist the help of friends to create your cover. This is likely to be the most complex and expensive.

Option 1 – KDP Cover Creators

Amazon's Kindle Direct Publishing offers a cover creator for both the Kindle and paper editions that let you add your own material to your choice of pre-designed templates. You can use your paper cover for your Kindle edition or use the Kindle cover as the start of your paper cover and add the back cover material. The cover creators give you the option of uploading your own photographs, etc. and are quite flexible. Either way, the publishing platform is making your cover for you. Free.

This is a simple and low-stress approach. You are guaranteed a workable, attractive cover. If you are publishing both a paper book and a Kindle book, your simplest option is to use the cover creator and let Amazon transfer the cover to the other publishing platform for you. You only make one cover that way, and it gets used for both editions.

You are introduced to the KDP cover creator part way through the KDP publishing process, after you have filled in basic information about the book. It is at the same place in the process as the place where you upload the formatted book text, so you can upload the book then work on the cover while the book is undergoing its initial review.

Basically, the cover creator offers you a choice of preformatted templates, and allows you to make limited selections of colors, fonts, etc. For the paper book, it provides a place for you to insert a promotion for the book or a description, a biography of yourself, and photographs.

If you decide to go with the cover creator, be prepared to spend a little time with it. It is a relatively simple process, but it rewards thoughtfulness, and you will still need to make some artistic decisions and provide some text. What the cover creator does for you is provide templates that are going to be tasteful and workable, and guides you through the creation process.

There are minor format differences in the cover creator for soft cover and hard cover; the cover creators will guide you through whatever you need to do.

Hint; if you include a brief description of the book on the back cover and/or an author biography, you can use the same description and biography later on in the publishing process.

Keep in mind that the Kindle cover creator only creates the "front" cover; for the paper version, you will have to add that back cover material. It's not a big deal.

Option 2 – Create Your Own Cover

There are a range of possibilities here, from doing a from-scratch cover design to buying an inexpensive, pre-designed cover and integrating it into your front and back cover layout. You only need the front cover for Kindle books, so if it's a Kindle-only book, the pre-made cover requires a minimum of work, and gives you a unique design.

If you decide to create your own cover, either from scratch or by integrating a pre-designed cover into your front and back layout, you can use software you might already have to create the cover. It doesn't have to be "layout" software specifically; anything that meets the following criteria can work;

- It must let you define the page dimensions. You will need specific dimensions for the Kindle cover, and different dimensions that are dependent on the

number of pages for the paper book cover(s).
- It must be capable of placing text and images anywhere on the page.
- It has to offer control over the text; font, size, color, and the size of images.

If you have Illustrator, InDesign, PhotoShop, or something similar, you're in business. If not, then it's time to shop the internet. There is good software available that will do the job.

For PC's, Serif's Page Plus Starter Edition is free, powerful, and easy to use.

For Macs, try Scribus, a very powerful free alternative to InDesign, but be aware that the user interface can be maddening.

Hint; if you're working in Scribus, stick with measurements in points for document setup, otherwise it can have problems with exporting the right size.

If you don't mind spending a few dollars, the Mac-specific drawing program from Serif, Affinity Designer, is only about $50 from the app store and is amazingly powerful. If you have any ambitions towards graphic design, this is a good starting point. It's easily 90% the functionality of Illustrator, and less frustrating.

If you are doing both paper and Kindle books, make one and use it as the basis for the other so they'll be similar. And remember, it has to be legible when displayed the size of a postage stamp on Amazon.

As far as the actual front cover design, you're pretty much on your own for the artistic aspects. Photos work well, but they need to be good photos; they must attract the eye and say something about the book. If the book includes illustrations, one of them might be a good starting point for a cover. If you're using your own photo, be sure the resolution is up to the job; a minimum of 300 dpi. The usual cell phone photo or downloaded 72 dpi clip art won't work here, it'll look really awful.

Text on a design or colored background can be a safe choice. Plain text on a solid color can be a powerful statement, too, because it's unusual. White space is the most unusual of all. Pick color combinations that are readable, though. Black on white or black on yellow jumps out; red on blue is impossible to read (our eyes can't focus on both of those colors at once) and blue on green or yellow on white results in invisible text.

The idea is to catch the potential reader's eye and say something about the book. That's why six-pack abs, rockets and bombs, spaceships, etc. are featured on book covers; to tell the reader what to expect. You can do some basic research at the paperback rack in the local drugstore, or just browse your genre on Amazon and see what others are doing, and what catches your eye.

One possibility is to buy a front cover design from a site like *http://the-bookcoverdesigner.com*, which sells pre-made covers relatively inexpensively ($5 to $100), and integrate it into your front and back layout. You can then add your own title and text, or let the designer do it for you. You will spend a good bit of time looking at the pre-made cover designs, most of which won't be exactly what you had in mind, but you will get a custom cover at a very low price. In fact, you might get the designer to do the whole job, back cover included. This can be sort of a hybrid between doing your own and getting a custom professional cover design.

Creating a Kindle Cover

If you want to design your own cover, this is how to proceed. Open up whatever program you're using for cover design and layout and set up the document as follows;

- Set the height to the Kindle virtual trim height of 8.5."
- Set the width to 6.5." If you're working in pixels or points, set the dimensions to 2500 tall by 1600 wide at 300 dpi resolution.
- Set the margins to zero.
- Set your color space to RGB for now.
- Design your cover! Expect this to take a while, and involve many iterations. If you have already designed the paper cover, modify it to fit the Kindle parameters.

This may seem obvious, but the cover is where you want the title of the book, and your name.

Once you've uploaded the cover as a .jpg as described in the next chapter, you might want to come back and adjust the brightness and colors of the Kindle version after you see it go live. For the Kindle version, which will be viewed approximately postage stamp-size, you might also want to bump up the type size, depending on how easy it is to read on line. If this turns out to be the case, you might want to save a separate, Kindle-only version of your cover so you don't upset the artistic merits of the paper book cover.

That's it for the Kindle cover. You can, and should, however, use the same basic design for the paper book cover. You really want a connection between the two versions.

Creating the Paper Book Cover

The paper book cover is more complicated than the Kindle cover because the paper book cover requires you to do the front and back covers as a single layout, taking in to account the thickness of the book and the trim size. After reading this you may very well decide to stick with the KDP free cover.

To make it even more interesting, the dimensions and details of a hardback cover are subtly different from those of a soft cover.

If you are doing your own design you should use software that lets you place the cover elements anywhere on the page, and that lets you define the size of the page. Again, an illustration program is ideal for this work. Any software that will give you good freedom of placement and eventually export as a .pdf will work.

However you do it, start with the Kindle cover if you already have one and modify it to work for the paper cover.

By far the easiest way to create a soft or hard cover is to start with KDPs Cover Calculator. You enter your page count, paper type, and trim size into the Calculator and it generates both dimensions and templates for both types of covers. You can either download the template into your graphics program, or use the dimensions to create your own template.

For either cover, you need to start with the page count so you or the Calculator can calculate the thickness of the book and consequently the width of the front/spine/back cover. That is why the cover creation process is completed after the text is prepared and formatted. At this point you will have decided whether you will print on bright white or slightly off-white paper, as it makes a difference in thickness. If your book has any internal illustrations, you might prefer bright white; otherwise, the off-white can be easier on the eyes.

If you want to go through the process manually, calculate your book spine width for a paper cover, as follows;

- For white paper, black-and-white printing (no color inside at all), multiply the number of pages by 0.002252.
- For off-white, or cream, paper, black-and-white printing, multiply the number of pages by 0.0025.

- For books with color pages, multiply the page count by 0.002347.

This will be the width of the spine, in inches. For example, if your book has 120 black-and-white pages, and you're using cream paper, the spine width is 120 X 0.0025 = 0.3"; about half way between ¼" and 3/8." If your book has 425 color pages on white paper, the spine width is 425 X 0.002347 = 0.99," almost 1 inch. Try to be as exact as possible with this, especially if you plan to limit the front cover design to only the front cover, with nothing wrapping around to the spine or back. Small errors here will be very obvious. It's best to err in the direction of wrapping the front onto the spine, either all the way or just barely past the fold, rather than leaving a contrasting strip at the left edge of the front cover.

Life is slightly easier with a hard cover; just use KDP's Cover Calculator to calculate the dimensions of the front, back, spine, and the little folding gutters where the hard cover hinges, and don't bother with all the manual calculations. Or better, use the template.

Now you're ready to set up your cover. Here are the steps for a soft cover, without using the Calculator or a template —

- Set the height of the cover layout to the trim height plus 0.25," to allow for 0.125" (that's 1/8") bleed on top and bottom.
- The width of the cover layout should be twice the

trim width plus the spine width plus 0.25"; again to allow 0.125" bleed on each side. Remember, you are laying out the front and back covers at the same time.

- For a final trim size of 8.5" X 5.5" with a 0.375" (that's 3/8") spine, the outside dimensions of the cover layout will be – 0.125" + 5.5" + 0.375" + 5.5" + 0.125," or a total of 11.625" wide.
- The height will be 0.125" + 8.5" + 0.125," for a total height of 8.75."

Important! The front cover is on the right-hand side of the cover layout, spine (and hinges, if any) in the middle, and back cover on the left.

- Put non-printing guidelines on your layout so you know where the spine folds and edges of the pages are. Put a guideline 0.125" down from the top, 0.125" up from the bottom, 0.125" from the left edge, and 0.125" from the right. Put two more guidelines to mark the spine.
- You want to run your cover design all the way out to the edges, right to the outside edges of the 0.125" bleed spaces, but keep the important parts, such as the text, at least 0.250" inside the trim lines.
- Don't put anything important in the lower right corner of the back cover; KDP will insert the ISBN bar code here.

Or, just use KPD's Cover Calculator, which will give you all the dimensions. It's good to walk through the steps involved in calculating the cover dimensions because it will make it easier to find problems, but in general, you can trust the Cover Calculator to do it right.

There is no reason not to wrap the front cover design around the spine on to the back cover, or to create a second back cover design. There is also nothing wrong with white or solid color for the back cover. Unless the book is more than about 0.5" thick (about 150 pages), there won't be room for anything printed on the spine. You do want to be sure you don't wrap the front cover part way across the spine by accident, or slop slightly over on to the back cover, unless you mean it. This is important; precision here pays off in a more professional looking cover.

Hard covers are both easier and trickier. The hinge part where the cover folds and the wrap around part where the cover graphics wrap around to the inside are calculated based on trim size, paper type, and page count. Just use the Cover Calculator to calculate the dimensions and adjust the layout for the paper cover accordingly. You will end up adding somewhere close to an inch to the horizontal dimensions, depending on trim size, paper type and page count. The Cover Calculator will give you the details.

The rest of the back cover is up to you, but it's a terrific place to "sell" the book, so take advantage of it. An excerpt, a description, something that will make the browser open the book. A picture of you, and a very short biography, is one possibility. The back cover will not be seen by Amazon browsers, but it will be seen when the book is ordered by bookstores or delivered to readers, so take advantage of it.

As a final step, save the cover as a .pdf with a unique name. You will upload the paper cover as a .pdf, not a .jpg.

Option 3 – Professional Covers

You can advertise on Craigslist or the like, although this limits you to the local artistic pool. You can approach graphic arts students at the local community college; you might uncover the next big name in art this way. An advertisement posted on a bulletin board in the graphic arts area can be effective. Another way to find freelance graphic artists is through a web site such as *ifreelance.com* or *freelance-graphicartist.net*. Ask for samples of their work, and get a firm price quote. Remember, though, that they can't read your mind or predict the future; late changes in the design will cost money. Expect to spend at least $200 for a custom professional cover; it is very time consuming and requires a high degree of skill and training.

Once again, you might check with the designers at sites such as *http://the-bookcoverdesigner.com* for a complete, ready-to-go front and back cover design to your format specifications, either paper book or Kindle; or both. These sites specialize in covers designed by freelance graphic artists who post their designs for potential buyers and often will customize the design to suit. For example, the designer will generally offer to insert the book title and author name as part of the design service. The price for a complete custom layout will depend on how much work the designer has to do, but it will almost certainly be less expensive than a from-scratch custom cover.

One caveat; don't necessarily expect the cover designer to be familiar with the KDP formatting requirements. Either make that part of your deal, or plan on fiddling with the design yourself.

Summary

- The Kindle version cover has a rigid format unrelated to the trim size.
- The paper book cover includes spine and back cover, with dimensions depending on trim size and page count, as one document, with the "front" on the

right-hand side.
- Hard covers and soft covers have slightly different formatting requirements.
- The paper book cover, both hard and soft versions, must be in .pdf format, at least 300 dpi resolution.
- The Kindle cover must be in .jpg format, at least 300 dpi resolution.
- The easiest way for a new author is to use KDP cover creators.
- If you are publishing both a paper and Kindle version, create one cover and use it for both versions.

Common Problems

- Low resolution.
- Paper book front cover on left, incorrect side.
- Paper book cover not properly fitted to trim size; lapping over on to spine, etc.
- Wrong file formats - mind your .jpgs and .pdfs.
- Hard to read cover; mind the typeface and size!

Publishing

Log in to your KDP account and complete any information about the book that you haven't already filled in; title, author, description, category, key words, etc. Fill in all the blanks.

Description, Key Words, and Biography

This is important. You are going to create a description of the book, a brief author biography, select a category, and select key words. You can change any of these things later.

You have surely read many book descriptions; what appeals to you? If you were asked what your book is about while waiting in line at Starbuck's or the grocery store, what will you say? If your book is exciting, suspenseful, insightful, humorous, roll-on-the-floor funny, helpful, useful, entertaining, easy to read, biographical, filled with insider information, shocking, romantic; say so. Say it right away in the description. Only the first few lines of the description will appear on Amazon (until the reader clicks the "see more" button), so pack as much in to those lines as you can.

Here's a hint; you can include search terms in the description. If a potential reader is looking for a book about female plumbers with red hair, they will search on those terms. If your book is about Trixie, the redheaded plumber / spy, say so right up front. Help the reader find your book.

Again, see what other books like yours are using. Do a search on Amazon on a category that you might think fit and see what comes up. Those are not your competition; those are the books that will lead readers to yours.

Do a search on your categories on Google as well. The first few entries on a Google search (after the paid listings) are the ones that appear most frequently. Are those books similar to yours? You want a category (and keywords, described later) that gives you the maximum chance of being found by a search, which means you want a category and keywords that are commonly used as search terms.

Make your author biography interesting, short, relevant, and personal. If you are writing about cats, tell us how much you like your three cats, Momma, Scratches, and Puddles. If you are writing about the history of calculus instruction in private schools, let us know what possessed you to do such a thing. It is common to do the biography in the third person; for example, "Ms. Grinchwell taught typing and deportment to terrified 7th graders for 27 years." Talk about who you are, why you wrote this book, what it means to you. You are making a personal connection with the reader.

You are probably publishing in the United States, in English, but maybe not. Pick the location and language of publication on this page.

Key words are another potentially complicated area; again, search on Amazon on key words that you think might apply, see what comes up. That's where your book will appear. You can sneak key words into the description, so don't feel too limited by the fact that you are only allowed seven in KDP. You're more likely to have a hard time coming up with key words.

And if your book has what KDP is pleased to call "adult content" or is in large type, now is the time to point that out. By the way, large type books are not all that common, so if you have the skill and inclination, creating a separate large type edition might be worthwhile. I'm not going to deal with it here, though.

While you're at it, consider KDP Select. This program lets you use some of Amazon's marketing muscle. You can run periodic promotions and let your book appear in Amazon's book borrowing program (which pays a royalty, too). The only downside, if it is one, is that if it's in KDP Select, it can't be available as an electronic publication elsewhere, including your own blog site. Personally, I thing KDP Select is a pretty good deal because I'm too lazy to have a blog.

Remember that you can go back to the bookshelf at any time, and quit at any time, and change just about anything, so there is no need to rush through this. Take the time to read the underlined learn more links.

Upload your Kindle Book

I'm assuming you are doing the Kindle version first, in which case, upload your Kindle-specific interior file, either the .doc or the Kindle .kpf file you created earlier with Kindle Create. Once your files are uploaded, the previewer will appear. You can also download a previewer, but the on-line one is easy to deal with.

This is where you see, again, how your book will look on the several Kindle readers. I might be slightly different from what you saw in Kindle Create because now you're looking at the actual version that will go out to readers. Each reader formats the display differently; it will take a while to review the several versions. Pay particular attention to page breaks and strange symbols appearing where you intended a bullet or a line break. The Kindle conversion process attempts to filter out such things, but is not always successful. It may be necessary to go back to the manuscript or Kindle-specific file and replace bullets with dashes, or some similar strategy; or add or remove page breaks. Work towards a file that is acceptable on each of the Kindle readers. This may take a few tries. You get out of the on-line reviewer by clicking on the small, not-obvious book details tab in the upper left corner of the screen.

You can save everything as a draft at any time and come back later, or save and continue to the next step after you are satisfied with the interior files.

You can either create or upload your cover at this point. You need to have both the interior contents and the cover uploaded, reviewed, and approved by you before you can proceed beyond this point, but you can come back later if you discover a problem.

The next screen is where you set the distribution and selling price for your Kindle book, and enroll in two powerful marketing programs; MatchBook and Kindle Book Lending. MatchBook is a program that lets readers buy the Kindle book at a reduced price, or free, if they buy the paper version. Kindle Book Lending makes your book available to borrowers, and pays a royalty on the loan. Both programs are worth opting in to. Personally, I like to give away the Kindle version with the paper version; I believe it is a potential selling point.

KDP has a tool to suggest a selling price based on similar books, it's the View Service button, and it gives you a starting point, based on your categories and book size. Anything less than $2.99 pays a 35% royalty, anything between $2.99 and $9.99 pays 70%, subject to some terms regarding country of sale, delivery costs, etc. If you don't know what else to do, take the suggested price; you can always adjust it later.

We're not done. You have to accept the publication terms (a little box at the bottom of the page) before you can publish. You will be notified by e-mail when your book is available on Amazon; usually within 12 hours. At this point, you're finally done with the Kindle book and are ready to move on to the paper book. You can start on the paper book while you're waiting on the Kindle review process; they are independent of one another.

Upload Your Paper Book

Now you are ready to upload your paper book. KDP will offer you that option after you upload and complete the

Kindle book; take it. Most of the information you entered for the Kindle version will just transfer to the paper version. You will have the choice of hard cover or soft cover book.

As with the Kindle version, you are going to upload or create two files; the book interior, and the cover. I am assuming you are not using Kindle Create to make your final paper book file; if you are, then follow the directions it gives you. Otherwise, here's how you do it.

First, click on Upload your Book File. Use the Browse button to find your .pdf file and select it. The Upload window will say that it can accept .doc, .docx, .pdf, and .rtf files, or use your already-uploaded Kindle file. Don't believe it; it can make a real mess of a .doc file. It does best with .pdf. A .doc or .docx file with significant formatting will have problems in the translation, while a .pdf file is literally what will print.

Upload and save and you will get a progress bar and an automated print check message. This will take a few minutes. You will be invited to have a cup of coffee or start work on your cover in the meanwhile, so go ahead and either open up cover creator or upload your prepared cover.

The Cover

The Cover section is where you select the paper finish for your cover, hard or soft; glossy or matte. Glossy may do better with photographs but the matte finish is less likely to give you annoying reflections. Here's a tip; matte takes ink better, so it's easier to autograph. You have options for your cover, as we discussed in the chapter on covers.

If you choose to use the cover creator, just follow the instructions, it will walk you through the process. Again, you can come back at any time.

If you created your own cover, or had a freelance artist create it for you, select that option, upload a Print-Ready .pdf, and follow the on-screen directions. It can take a few minutes to upload the interior and cover files, so just be patient.

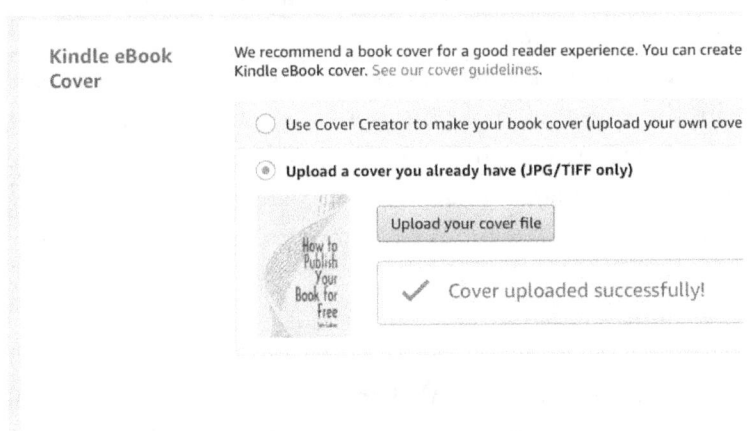

During the initial automated review of your newly-uploaded files you might get a message telling you that there was a problem with your files. The message will also tell you in general terms what the problems are, so you can fix them.

Once the initial automated review is complete, launch the Interior Reviewer. You will get an on-screen view of exactly how your book will look line in print. If you were tempted to upload a .doc or .docx file, this is where you will see how bad things can be, and why I recommend a .pdf.

Read every page as though you'd never seen it before. Also read the instructions for the interior reviewer, they are very helpful. As you find problems, note the page number and the nature of the problem. When you finish reviewing your book, click save and continue, and go back and make the changes to your manuscript so you can make another .pdf upload it again. You can close out the window while you do this; nothing gets lost and you can always go back to where you left off.

Keep reviewing and re-uploading until you are satisfied with the appearance of your book. This might take a few tries. There is no rush on this. You will have another chance at reviewing it later, and can make changes at any time, but you might as well get it as close to perfect as you can now.

Complete Setup

Once you have uploaded an interior file and a cover file, you can move on to completing the setup. This has two screens; File Review and Proof Your Book. File Review is where you submit your files for another review; this time by a combination of software and if necessary, humans. The process takes about a day, and you will be notified by email when the reviewed files are ready for your approval. Errors will be identified, if any. Sometimes, the automated review process will identify errors that aren't really errors, like differences in color space that might not matter to you. You must then Proof Your Book again on the next screen.

You can proof the book on line, which is a speedy and free option, not really different from reading your manuscript as you've been doing for all this time. Familiarity might lead you to overlook some problems, though. You can also download a .pdf of the final book to read. Reading on paper is different somehow. A great choice is to pay the modest fee (generally less than $10) to have a printed proof copy mailed to you via priority mail. It takes about a week to arrive. There is nothing quite like holding the first printed copy of your book in your hand. This is where you will find those errors that escaped your attention through the several on-screen reviews.

If you are happy with the book, you can go to the Review tab, and approve the book for publication. It will ask you twice if you approve.

You can also go back yet again and upload a revised interior file or change your cover. Each time, you will have to go through the submittal and review process, and review and approve the final book before it can be published. For minor changes the on-screen reviewer is pretty reliable.

The key takeaway here is that you can keep iterating submission-review-resubmission until you are satisfied.

Once you have approved your book, you can next move on to the Distribute tab. This is where you select distribution channels, set a price, and otherwise take care of the commercial aspects. This is also where you do some other, very important things.

Categories and Description

You might want to select all of the distribution channels. This makes your book available through Amazon, bookstores, and libraries. There is no direct charge for opting for the widest possible distribution.

However, the distribution you select does affect the cost to Amazon and therefore the selling price. If you select Expanded Distribution, which includes commercial book distribution channels, the minimum selling price will increase because distribution costs increase. For the lowest possible selling price, stick with Amazon, and omit Expanded Distribution. If you expect sales to bookstores, then select Expanded Distribution. You can change this at any time.

Save and Continue, and move on to the next screen where you set a price for the book. Amazon will calculate the minimum selling price based on printing and shipping costs with little or no royalty to you. You obviously want to charge a bit more than the minimum, but how much?

Setting the cost is tricky; if it is too low, then it gives the appearance that you do not value it. If it is too high, it may be priced out of the market. One approach is to do a little research on Amazon to see what similar books sell for. If you have a historical romance novel of 100,000 words and most others are selling for $9.95, with a few at $7 and a few at $17, and Amazon calculates the minimum cost at $7, set your price around that average price of $9.95, give or take a dollar or so. Give yourself a reasonable royalty. You earned it. You can always adjust the price later, but it's easier to reduce it than to increase it.

Now submit it for review and you're almost done.

There is one more step. As with the Kindle book, KDP will email you in about 24 hours to tell you that your book is approved and is available.

Congratulations! You're a published author! Now, let's tell people about it.

Marketing

You want people to know about your book so they will read it. That means you have to tell people about it.

First, though, a reality check. You may not be an overnight sensation. Shocking, yes. Your book will get published, and people will read it, but with literally millions of published works appearing each year, the element of chance plays a large role in determining what books become incredibly popular and what books enjoy limited circulation. Some truly awful stuff somehow gets mentioned by Oprah or hits the New York Times best seller list, while a lot of gems go unnoticed. If you do not achieve instant fame, it's not because your book is no good, it's just that nobody knows about it. Let's maximize your exposure.

Your publicity efforts have two goals.

- You want to get the word out about your book to as many potential readers as possible; to create a buzz, and
- You want to promote your brand. You want to become interesting, talked about, read because you're you.

Let's look at some common strategies.

News Release

Really; this works, for both paper books and Kindle. Newspapers are always looking for news, and especially local news. Send a 100–200 word press release to your local newspaper(s). Emphasize your local-ness, that's what they want to see. Write it in the third person, expand on your author biography, tell people a little bit about the book, and, very important, how they can get your book. Be sure and include the title! If nothing else, your name will appear in the paper.

Does your newspaper have a gossip columnist, an arts editor? Send them a copy of your book.

Similarly, if there is a local TV program that fills up air space in the early morning with gossip, weather, celebrity news, and interviews, contact them. They are probably begging for something interesting to talk about. Send them a free copy. You may or may not go anywhere with it, but hey, it's publicity. They might even invite you to appear.

FaceBook and other Social Media

Set up an author page on FaceBook, dedicated to your writing, and promote it, a lot. Don't waste time with things like the "50 guaranteed FaceBook 'like' pictures," we've all seen them and don't like them all that much. Instead, post cheerful and personal things. It's nice if they are somehow related to your book or to you, but not totally necessary. Everyone will "like" a rainbow.

Twitter! Say interesting things, get followers. Get more followers. You already know how to say interesting things.

Amazon Free Books

"Free" is hard to resist. Kindle Select has two free promotional schemes; one allows you to give away your Kindle book for up to 5 days in a 90 day period, the other is a "countdown" deal where the price changes daily (and which is, frankly, not as interesting). Go with the free books option.

Why should you give away your book? Because you want reviews; lots of reviews. It costs you nothing. Amazon's algorithms for suggesting things for people to read are based on a book's popularity. The more readers, the more likely it is to be promoted by Amazon. The more reviews, the more likely it is to be promoted. The higher it is in sales rankings, even for a day, the more likely it is to be promoted. The more it is promoted, the more it will sell. You can boost all three with a couple of days of giveaways, if you manage it right.

This means promoting the giveaway. One way to promote the giveaway is on Face-book. Post it a couple of times a day, starting a couple of days before the giveaway, and include a link to the Amazon page where the book is sold.

Hint; you can use a website like tinyurl.com to make a short version of the page address for the link.

You can also use Face-book's post promotion scheme; $10 worth of promotion will send your post to about 4,000 Face-book people. This is a pretty good reach, but it can be expensive.

You can also promote the giveaway with a mass mailing, but it takes a bit more work. *MailChimp.com* is very effective for mass mailings, as is *Vertical Response.com*.

MailChimp and Vertical Response are email management websites that let you build a newsletter-format emailing and send it to your mail list. MailChimp is not a particularly user-friendly site; some of the operations are not obvious, and it costs money. Vertical Response is free for small mail lists and is easier to navigate. Once you have an account and mail list set up, it is relative easy to send out notices of upcoming promotions from either site. Another bonus is that you can encourage readers to sign up for your MailChimp or Vertical Response mailings by including a link to your mail list in your personal emails.

Importing email addresses into MailChimp is a special kind of annoying. For Mac users the pain is eased with an app called, appropriately, Chimport, which takes your Contacts list and converts it to a MailChimp format. Vertical Response is easier and the instructions are clearer.

However you can get the word out, Amazon free book giveaway is an effective way of building a readership. It is not unusual to give away hundreds of copies of a Kindle book in a single day, just from a couple of Face-book post-ings and a MailChimp mailing to a list of about 100. This means that those people who saw your Face-book or MailChimp shared it with others. This is what you want.

A few hundred copies in a day is generally enough to make you #1 or #2 seller that day in your category, which means that you automatically rise a bit in Amazon's esteem. It also means that you might garner a couple of reviews, which you really want.

You get to the book giveaway by clicking on the pro-mote and advertise button for your book in your KDP bookshelf; the first thing to greet you is Tools to Promote Your Book, where the giveaway is managed.

Friends and Relatives

Bribe, beg, whine, cry, whatever it takes. Get your friends and relatives to write you a review. Get them to share your postings, your Tweets, your promotional emails. Bake them a cake, promise them a trip to Disneyland, free babysitting. Be shameless. Reviews and book sales (including giveaways) bump you up in the Amazon recommendation universe, and that's how you get readers.

Paid Promotion Through Amazon

Amazon also offers a paid promotion scheme, Amazon Marketing Services. That's the other button on the Tools to Promote Your Book screen. This is a little more complex.

Basically, you "bid" to have your book promoted when a potential reader goes to look at another, similar book. The similarity can be either by category or by specific title. You set a maximum bid (maybe 5¢ per click through) and a budget (minimum $100) and duration (1 month is the default). It's potentially expensive; all the previous tools are free.

The good news is that if you pay for $100 dollars worth of 5¢ click-throughs (that's 2000 click-throughs) and sell even 5% of that many books, that's 100 books sold. The royalties will be much more than the cost of the click-throughs. In real life, though, you might get a few dozen to a hundred clicks, but it's still a good deal if you sell a few books.

Book Stores

This is a mixed bag. Small independent bookstores frequently host local authors to talk about their books or whatever might be interesting. The author generally signs books after; books are sold by the bookstore. This will get your name out (the book store will promote the talk), sell a few books, but you won't make anything because the book store will take 50% or more of the cover price, and chances are you have to buy the books yourself and let the bookstore sell them and take their cut. If your book retails for $7, the bookstore takes half, and your cost per copy from KDP is $4, you lose 50¢ per copy. You might negotiate a better deal, such as breaking even. You are not going to make much money this way, but you will reach some new readers and have fun at it.

If you are even a little tempted, do it. Having attended a few of these, I can tell you that even the worst presentation is more compelling than anything on television. It will work. If nothing else, read a few pages and answer questions. You can do that, right?

Amazon Author Page

Amazon will encourage you to create an Author Page. Why not? It's a place to blog, list your books, get comments, etc. No cost. One thing to be aware of; the biography on the Author Page will override whatever biography you attach to individual books. You might want to just use one biography for everything if you do an Author Page. It's free, and takes virtually no time or effort on your part. Why not do it?

Web Site

I have many friends who are artists. They tell me that never have they actually sold anything through their web site. I don't know about authors, but I suspect that until you get to superstar, or at least star, status, a web site is essentially like a business card; a way to introduce yourself. Still, it's a way to promote your "brand."

Building and hosting a basic web site through, for instance, *GoDaddy.com*, will cost you about $150 a year. Conventional wisdom is to at least buy your domain name; if your name is Barbara Smith, buy the domain name *Barbarasmith.com*. That's only about $15/year, and you can set up a web site later, if you want. There are a couple of dozen web site hosts more than happy to sell you a domain name and host your web site. *GoDaddy.com* and *Squarespace.com* are two popular ones, or your local ISP might offer you a good deal.

Unless you are good at it, maintaining a web site can be tedious, although you can use the site to host your blog. If you really want a web site, though, you can use it to appear bigger and more famous by using the mail service provided by the web site (at extra cost, usually) as your routine email address. It will look something like *Barbara@barbarasmithwrites books.com*. If nothing else, this lets everybody you correspond with know that you have a web site, and that you're an author. Brand building, again. Of course, you can also create *barbarasmithauthor@hotmail.com* and achieve a similar effect for free. The name-author thing in the address is like grill marks on a steak; it's a brand, distinguishes it from all the rest.

This is a good idea anyway, the separate email address for your author persona. Amazon has no problem letting you create a KDP account under a separate email address, different from your "normal" Amazon account, and you can use the separate, author address in your books as a way for your fans to communicate with you. If you get a stalker or something, you can just dump that address and work it out with Amazon.

Speaking of email, put a promotional plug in your personal email as your signature! Include a link to your book, maybe a really brief description. Again, everybody you email will get a little hint. It's easy to do, and is a constant reminder.

Business Cards

I have no real information as to how successful this is in selling books. I suspect pretty good, and I do know it's a sure-fire conversation starter. *VistaPrint.com*, for one, will make up custom business cards for $20 or so for 500 (they are always having some kind of deal). *Costco.com* has a similar deal. You could also do postcards or display cards, but they cost more and you aren't as likely to have a bunch in your pocket all the time. Plus, there's something inherently clever about the business cards. You can put your book cover, or the title, or just about anything related to the book on a business card (definitely mention how to get your book) and pass them out like candy at a Christmas parade. You can go through 500 cards pretty quickly.

Tack them to bulletin boards, leave them casually on the table when you eat out, hand them to people you meet. People you already know, too. It's cheap, easy, and actually fun. Be prepared to talk about your book. You should be prepared anyway; have an elevator sound byte ready, 20 seconds of what your book is about. Pretend the TV news lady, the one with the big hair, is interviewing you, which she actually might.

(Shoving a microphone in your face) "Tell the viewers a little bit about your book."

You now have between 10 and 20 seconds to be interesting. Should be no problem.

Blogging

This is yet another way of being interesting, of promoting your brand, without a hard sell. There are a couple of popular, free blog platforms – Blogger and Wordpress, to name two – that provide free, easy-to-use blog platforms. And, of course, you can use the blogging feature of your Amazon author page. Thanks to the internet, you will attract people who want to read you, and who will in turn tell others. And, of course, you can promote your blog on Facebook and Twitter.

The big downside to blogging is that you have to keep at it; a once-in-a-great-while blog entry does no good. People read blogs for entertainment value, like the newspaper comics and editorials. If we don't see them regularly, we lose interest. So, you have to commit to a regular, frequent blog schedule, and you have to be interesting. We already know you can be interesting; after all, you just wrote a book. If you can commit yourself to a regular blog "appearance," why not? Worst case, you lose interest and nothing happens.

You will think of other ways to publicize your book and build your reputation; these are but a few of the common ones. Go to it! Success really depends on you.

Details

In the interest of simplicity we skipped through a few things that you might be interested in, so I'll fill them in now.

About File Formats

Throughout the book I have referenced file formats with funny names; .doc, .docx, .jpg, .pdf, .png. The meaning of "file format" may not be clear to everybody.

By "file format" I mean the way in which the file is saved and consequently what software can read the file. This is indicated by the file extension; those three or four letters after the "." The three (or sometimes four) letters after the period in the file name are the extension; in the file named mybook.doc, the extension is .doc, which tells us that the file can be read by any program that can read a file with the extension ".doc." This format, or the similar .docx, is usually created by Microsoft Word, but is a near-universal format for word processor documents and can also be created, and read, by many other word processors.

Similarly, a file format indicated by the extension .pdf is a "portable document format," and can be read by many programs, since it was designed to be a near-universal read-only format (that is, you cannot easily change a .pdf file. It's possible, but not a simple thing.)

A .jpg format and the similar .png format are usually photographs or similar illustrations, and are also created by and readable by many programs that work with photos or illustrations. There are others such as .tiff and .psd, but .jpg is by far the most common.

Some formats are not easily readable by software other than that which created them; for example, the .indd file created by Adobe InDesign is for the most part not readable by any other software.

If your word processor is capable of exporting or saving in .doc format (that is, saving a file with the extension .doc), you can publish a Kindle book, either by uploading it directly or running it through Kindle Create to convert it to a native Kindle format document. Other formats nominally acceptable to Kindle can be unreliable in the conversion process, particularly if the book is anything but plain text with absolutely no adornments, typeface or style changes, although photos generally survive just fine. Kindle has real problems with .pdf files.

Similarly, if you can export or save to a .pdf format (on a Mac, you can "print" to save as a .pdf), you can publish a paper book on KDP.

ISBN

The ISBN – International Standard Book Number – is a unique identifying number, sort of like a serial number. You must have one. Surprisingly, the number itself is complicated, but easy to get.

You can buy your ISBN from several sources. The official US ISBN agency, ISBN.org, sells ISBNs for $125 each, which is hardly free.

The ISBN that KDP assigns for free is a little different; you can read about the details on the ISBN page on KDP, but basically, if you go for the KDP-assigned ISBN, you are committed to KDP for that ISBN; you cannot use it with another publisher, and KDP becomes the imprint of record. If you choose to publish this same book through another publisher, you will need another ISBN. You have the option, too, of buying an ISBN through KDP. There are some advantages in buying an ISBN; for one thing, you own everything about your book, lock, stock and barrel. On the other hand, if you do not anticipate another publisher, the Amazon-assigned ISBN is a bargain at the low, low price of free.

Does this mean that you cannot re-issue your book through another publisher? You will have to acquire a new ISBN, but you always own the intellectual property rights. So the free ISBN ties you to Amazon for that particular edition, but you are not tied forever.

Similarly, Kindle books have their own ISBN, but you don't need to worry about it because the Kindle book is tied to Amazon and can't be re-assigned. You can, of course, reformat to publish on, for example, NOOK, but that becomes a different book, at least as far as ISBNs are concerned.

Copyright

A copyright means that you own the intellectual property rights to what you have created; it cannot be copied by another and represented as their own work, and any use or quotations other than brief quotations for reviews or the like is illegal. As soon as the work is created, it is yours. The act of writing down your book creates ownership.

Copyright is automatic; you own it as soon as you create it. On the other hand, you don't have a really firm legal position as to when exactly it was created. This is where the process of registering a copyright comes into play. Registering your work with the U.S. Copyright Office (copyright .gov) is in itself legal proof of ownership, and is necessary if you intend to bring a lawsuit. The good news is that you can register up to 5 years after creation and still have that legal protection of creation time. The current application fee is $35, for which you get a nifty certificate of registration, suitable for framing. That in itself might be sufficient reason to register your book.

Book Formats

This book was formatted to match the KDP pre-made template for its trim size. It's a good, workable, streamlined format, commonly used for independently published work. Emphasis here is on "streamlined." You can get a lot more elaborate with the formatting.

The KDP templates put the title at the top of the page, centered; the page number at the bottom, centered; assumes a simple typeface, justified; and generally avoids complication. One common variation is to have the author name as one of the headers, or the chapter title. Page numbers can be offset to one side or another, at the top or bottom. You can use the margins as a design element. Conventional book publishing can include many more pages in the front matter and back matter. Book design is a complex art form in itself.

I assume here that you are primarily interested in getting your book into print, rather than focusing on the intricacies of publishing. The KDP template is a good, commonly-used starting point, just as the KDP cover is a good, workable cover if you are not inclined to create your own. You will inevitably learn much more about books and publishing as you progress; this is a starting point, not the final word on publishing.

About Type

I keep recommending common typefaces such as Times Roman, and speak of points and other typographic terms. Without getting too involved, I just want to point (pun intended) out that there are literally tens of thousands of typefaces; choice of typeface for a printed work is one more factor in book design. Generally, though, common serif faces such as Times Roman and Garamond are easy to read and are suitable for most books (a serif typeface is one with the little straight lines, or serifs, at the ends of the letters;

look at the bottom of the letters "l," "r," "m" for examples of serifs). Common sans-serifs (without the serifs) are good for things viewed on a screen. Helvetica and Arial are probably two of the most common sans-serif typefaces. The paper version of this book is set in 12 point Garamond. The Kindle version is whatever your reader thinks it should be, but it's probably some variation of Times Roman.

A point is a unit of measure used by printers since time immemorial. There are, unfortunately, slightly differing definitions, but the common usage today is that a point is 1/72 of an inch. Type size is measured in points, with more points meaning bigger type, but it is not an easy or obvious measurement since it is tied to the size of the metal block that used to be used to set type, not to the letter height itself; consequently, a the height of a nominal 12 point type size may vary from typeface to typeface. As a rough rule, the point size will be about the height of a capital letter.

This is 14 point Garamond.

This is 12 point Times Roman.

And this is 14 point Times Roman.

See the differences? Not if you're reading the Kindle version, which makes my point about typeface pretty clear. The Kindle book reader can and will change the typeface and size (although Times Roman or a similar serif font is the usual default). There are ways of forcing special fonts to appear, but it takes some trickery, and probably isn't worth the bother.

By the way; "typeface" refers to the design of the type, such as Times, Helvetica, etc. "Font" is the place the type is kept, not the name of the type, although the two terms are often used interchangeably. A minor. but to me annoying, point.

Kindle Tools

For e-books that are mostly text, Kindle Create, available from KDP, takes your Word manuscript and adds a table of contents, along with some very minor formatting. There is also a Kindle Create add-in for Word for PCs that does a bit more formatting. The finished product can be used to make both an e-book and a paper book, but be aware that you do not have complete freedom of formatting with Kindle Create. It is a very limited tool. Graphics, illustrations, etc. might not per presented quite how you wanted. The resulting document is a reflowable e-book file; that is, the book automatically adjusts width, breaks, etc. to fit the display.

If you are writing a book that is mostly or all text, Kindle Create and Word might be all you need. Kindle Create or its Word add-in can nearly-seamlessly turn your manuscript into a Kindle e-book; and the Word document, exported as a .pdf, is all you need for the paper version (and a cover, of course).

Kindle Textbook Creator, also from KDP, is a very powerful tool; used in its most basic manner, it turns your .pdf file that you made for KDP into a fixed, non-flowing e-book that is an exact replica of your paper book. Each page of the e-book is essentially a snapshot of the pdf page. The text does not adjust to the display device; rather, the whole display picture grows or shrinks to fit the screen. This static display is a critical difference from the more common re-flowable e-books.

Flowing and non-flowing might be a bit confusing. "Flowing" means the amount of material on the page automatically adjusts to the size of the reader page. There will be fewer words on the screen of a cell phone than on a tablet because the cell phone screen is smaller. This is what you want, usually, for a Kindle book. Non-flowing means the amount of material on the Kindle page is static; essentially, it is a picture of the page. The page on a cell phone and the page on a tablet will be identical except for the size. This is usually not what you want because it gets pretty hard to read when it's small.

Word Ninja Training

Let's face it; book design is complicated, and a lot of the design elements are just traditional things we do because we've always done them. Worse, "tradition" is not necessarily fixed; different designers have different ideas, so no two books will necessarily share exactly the same layout.

It's hard enough writing a book, proofreading it, and getting it ready to publish without adding layers of complexity. In this book I've tried to simplify things by presenting a basic design approach that includes the elements found in nearly all books since sometime around the 18th century, but I've omitted some of the finer points. For one thing, Word is not the most subtle tool for complex design (Kindle Create is even less flexible). For another, most of the time a lot of these things just don't matter.

Now, fasten your seat belt, because you are about to get familiar with some things that will make your life easier and let you enhance your book with all the whistles and bells your heart desires (almost).

This is not a detailed tutorial on Word; that is way outside the scope of this book. Community college courses may take two whole semesters to really dig into the things Word can do. Here is a quick guide to some tricks that will make your design more professional while letting you keep your sanity. In the interest of keeping it relatively simple, I'm ignoring a lot of the things you can do in Word. Keep in mind, too, that there is generally more than one way to do a thing.

I'm assuming you are using a recent version of Word, such as Office 2019. Many of the things we'll be doing can be done in Pages, Open Office, and in earlier versions of Word, but you'll have to find the right menus yourself. I'm focusing on the Mac version of Office 2019 because, well, I use a Mac and I believe it's the best tool for layout, but you PC people have all the same tools available and for a wonder, the menu bar is nearly identical.

Another caution before we begin. If you really, really want ultimate control over your layout, or if it includes things like full page bleeds or two-page spreads of photos or upside-down and backwards text wrapped in a spiral, you may not be able to do it in Word. People spend literally years getting familiar with professional layout programs like InDesign and QuarkXpress just so they can do these things. If book design catches your fancy, you might want to look into real, professional software; in some ways, it's easier than Word for many things.

Styles

You've already been introduced to styles, but let's refresh. At the top right of the menu bar is a box labeled "Styles Pane." Click on it to open up the styles palette. Older versions turn on the styles palette in one of the drop down menus, and it can open as a default. One of the "features" of the new Word is that you have to turn it on every time. Let's hear it for progress!

A style is a specific combination of typeface, spacing, indentation, and lots of little details that apply to whatever text you want it to. You should use a single style for all of the "normal" text in your book. It will make your life easier if you decide at the last minute to change right-justified Palatino into left-justified Garamond. Or pretty much anything else. Done right, you can change attributes of all the text in a given style by just changing it in the style.

Use a single style for your normal text, another style for chapter titles and nothing else, and other styles where you need to, but keep the number of styles under control. If you have more than three or four, ask yourself, why? Even the most complex technical document formats seldom use more. A style for text (and you can italicize, bold, super- and subscript within that style, no need for a separate one unless you really want it), a style for chapter titles, a style for footnotes and/or end notes, maybe a style for some front matter, maybe a style for the table of contents; that's pretty much it. You don't need to create a new style for the occasional italics, bold, or whatever.

If, on the other hand, you're working on your instruction manual for flux capacitor maintenance and suddenly think to yourself, "A poem would be good right here!" then by all means create a new style for flux capacitor poems if that will help. The point is, make your style choices manageable.

An easy way to create a new style is to simply type something in the typeface, indent, etc. that you want, then click on "new style." Word can pick up what you've done and create a new style from your example. Give it a name, something helpful like "book text," that explains what it is, and adjust it to suit. You can pick a typeface and size that you like, and change it in everything done in that style, any time you want. Be sure and select "Add to quick style list" at the bottom of the dialogue box so the style will appear in the styles pane.

There will be a lot of pre-defined styles in the styles pane. Ignore them. None of them will be helpful to you.

Now for more pro tips.

Click on "Format" at the bottom of the style pane and select "Paragraph." That brings up a menu for Indents and Spacing. Most books are designed with the space between lines, or "leading," at 120% of the typeface size. That is, if you are using 12 point type, the spacing will be 120% of that, or 14.4 points. Chances are, you created your manuscript double spaced, which looks amateur when it's published, or single spaced, which is hard to read. Let's fix that.

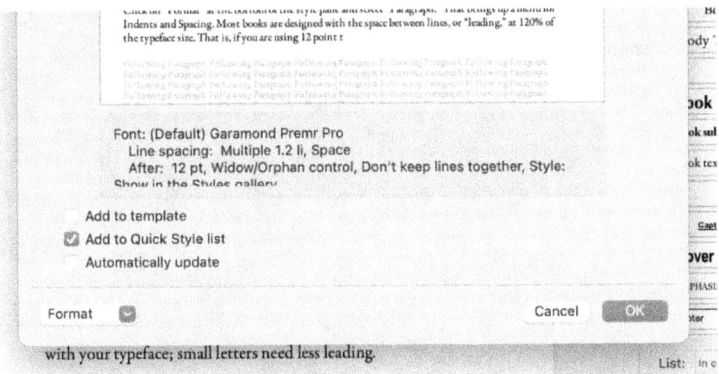

In the "Spacing" part of the paragraphs menu are the usual choices for indents and spacing between paragraphs. You also can define the line spacing, or leading, in terms of the typeface size, or just about anything else. If you select "Multiple" and set it at 1.2, the spacing will automatically be 120% of the typeface size. Anything between 1.1 and 1.35 will look good in print. Just make it work with your typeface; small letters need less leading.

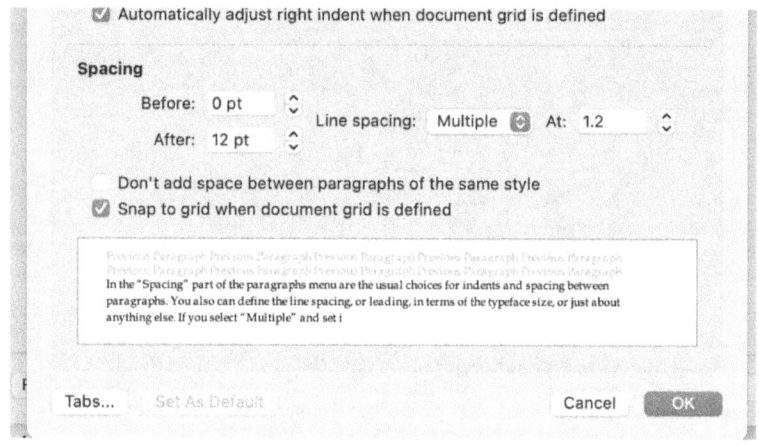

This dialogue box is also where you decide on indents and whether or not you'll have a space between paragraphs. Do one or the other; not both.

By the way, the other "Paragraph" tab, "Line and Page Breaks'" has a handy little tool to make sure you don't start a new page with one word, or other awkwardness. It's "Widow/Orphan control" and you want it checked. It will keep you from having a page start with one word and things like that. Keeping all the lines of a sentence together can result in some really awkward-looking pages, so just stick with "Widow/Orphan control" for now.

You can also set tabs for the style you're using, although that's not likely to be something you'll need. We won't worry about the other dialogue boxes in a style, that's enough complication for now

Sections

Sections are a powerful tool, and an easy way to make a mess. Basically, a section is a break in the layout where anything and everything–except styles–can change. You can restart page numbers, change from single column to multi-column layout, change margins; just about any of the text characteristics. You can even change page size, although that would be pretty unlikely in a book. Hard to print, for one thing. So, you need to know about sections. Here's why.

To recap again, something professionally-designed books do is to not have headers and footers in the front matter. They also begin the text of the book itself on the right-hand, odd-numbered page, right after the front matter. That first page of text is a new section and does not usually have a number or a header or footer on it. That requires a minimum of two sections; one for front matter, without headers and footers, and a second section for the text itself, with headers, footers, and page numbers. If you have appendices, an afterword, or other back matter, that might be yet another section. The pre-defined templates include separate sections for most of the front matter pages and for each chapter. You definitely need to be able to manipulate these, if only to delete some of them.

For example, books also usually begin each subsequent chapter on a right-hand, odd-numbered page. This sometimes means inserting a blank facing page, with no text, header, or footer. You could, of course, just stick in an extra page break, but that blank page will have the header and footer of all the other pages. Another way is to start a new section for the blank page, then another new section for the next chapter, and so on. There's one use for sections.

You add a section by going up to "Insert" on the menu bar and clicking "Break," then "Section break" on the next menu. Ignore the other options for now. You can also do it in the "Layout" tab; "Breaks" is about 1/3 of the way from the left of the ribbon.

Bookmark...	arting with "ii" on
Cross-reference...	mbers starting wit
Comment	e back matter to l
	three sections.
Break ▶	nts can set your v
Footnote...	Kindle Create. H
Caption...	parate style for ch;
Index and Tables...	of editing after y
Watermark...	
Page Numbers...	
Text Box ▶	
AutoText ▶	
Date and Time	

If you mess up, you get rid of a section break by going into "View," "Draft," or turn on the reveal formatting symbol (a little thing that looks like a backwards letter "P") and command-clicking on the section break to delete it. That's a right-click for you PC people.

Now, that blank page will not have page numbers, headers, footers, or anything else unless you say so. Double click in the header area and it will bring up the header/footer editing tools. See the box that says "link to previous?" Uncheck it. You'll have a blank page, no headers or footers.

The downside to this is that you have to re-create the header, footer, and page number on the next section, where you start the next chapter.

That can be quite a bit of work, and you might not want to go through all the fiddling with sections to get blank pages, re-starting page numbers, and so forth. Do not despair! A reasonable compromise, one I have generally advocated, is to either start from scratch and make a template yourself, or simply delete most of the sections in the downloaded template, and make blank pages where you need them by adding a page break. I talked about this in the chapter on formatting.

You still want at least two sections. You can put the front matter in one section of blank pages, no headers or footers, and manually insert Roman numeral page numbers, and a second section for the body of the text, with have headers and page numbers starting with "2" on the second page.

You create a page number by clicking in the header or footer area, where ever you want the page numbers, and opening up the "Page Number" tool on the left edge of the ribbon. It has lots of options for placement. You can assign a style to page numbers, too. You tell Word what you want the first page number to be, and whether or not you want a page number on the first page of the section. Usually not.

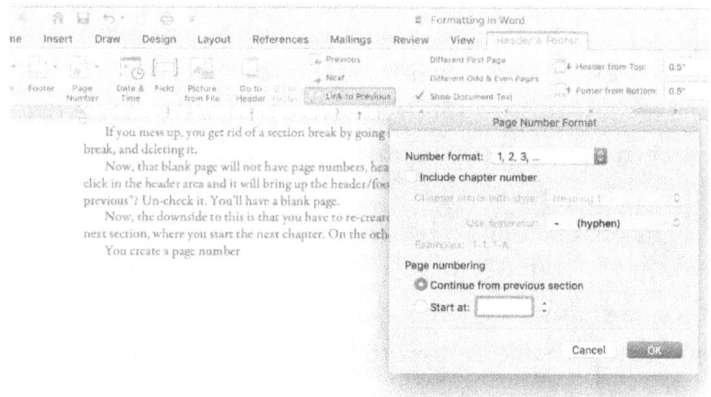

How hard was that? OK, it was not obvious.

You can have a lot of sections if you are using the pre-defined template as-is. That's why pros use layout software that does a lot of these things automatically. On the other hand, the cost of some of that software would buy a pretty decent car, and require maybe a year or two of training, so there're trade-offs in everything.

Headers and Footers

Word's treatment of headers and footers can sometimes be awkward; anything in a header or footer will appear on every page until you change the header or footer in the next section. You have the option of leaving them off of the first page of a section, but otherwise, you're stuck. You can, however, have different headers or footers on odd and even pages. Some designers will put the book title on one side and the author's name on the other. Sometimes, the chapter title will be in one or both headers, which obviously means creating a new header for each section.

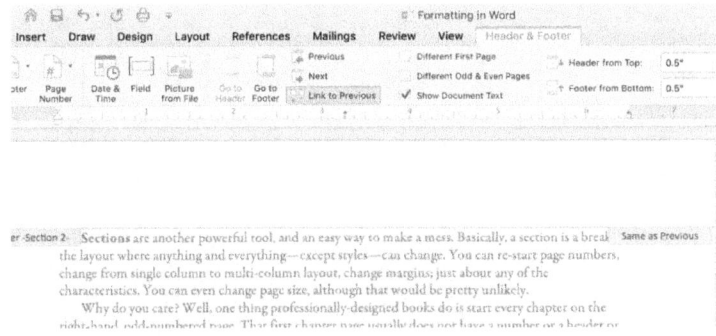

Alignment

The pre-defined templates start with some text centered, top to bottom, in some places where you don't want it to be. In the "Layout" tab, on the right side, is an "Align" icon. Select the text you want to adjust and click how you want it aligned. Generally, "Align Top" is a good choice for everything. If you want a text block centered on the page, as for an acknowledgement, select it and click "Align Center."

Sometimes this option is greyed-out. In that case, go to "File-Page Setup," then at the top where it says "Page Attributes" click on the arrows until you get "Microsoft Word." "OK" will bring up another dialogue box for "Margins." That's the one you want to change the vertical alignment and other things. It's in the "Layout" tab and can apply to a section, or the whole document. You can also change header/footer sizes and page numbers here.

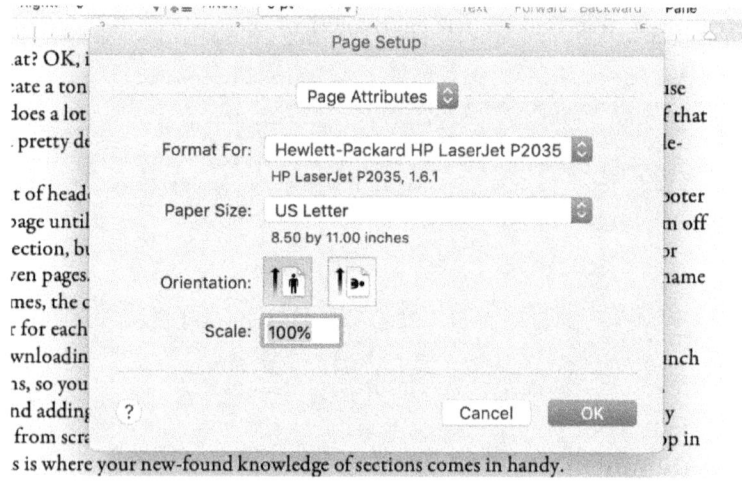

Page Setup

Microsoft Word

Apply Page Setup settings to: Whole Document

Margins...   Default...

?   Cancel   OK

you get "Microsoft Word." "OK" will bring up another

Margins and Page Size

I've already addressed margins and page size, but here it is again. In "Layout," at the left edge, you set the page size icon, none of which choices are likely to be what you want. Instead, go to "File" in the top menu bar, "Page setup" near the bottom. It will bring up your printer dialogue box. Where it says "Paper size," select "Manage Custom," which brings up another menu where you can enter the trim size of your book. The example is for 5 ½ " X 8 ½", a common trim size.

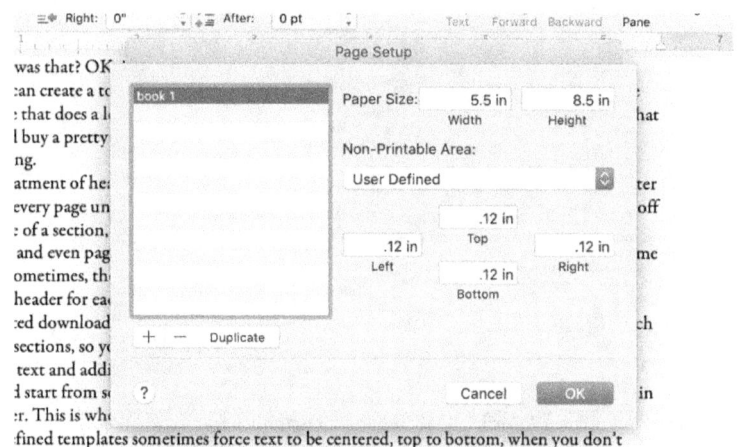

Margins are easy. "Layout," "Custom Margins." More choices. Of course, you can also set the margins by sliding the little indicators along the ruler at the top. "Mirrored" is a good default for most books. Allow some room for binding; the "gutter." You can also adjust header and footer settings in the "Custom Margin" dialogue box. Make your margins a reasonable portion of the page dimensions, 10% to 20% of the page width and height, with the bottom a bit bigger than the top.

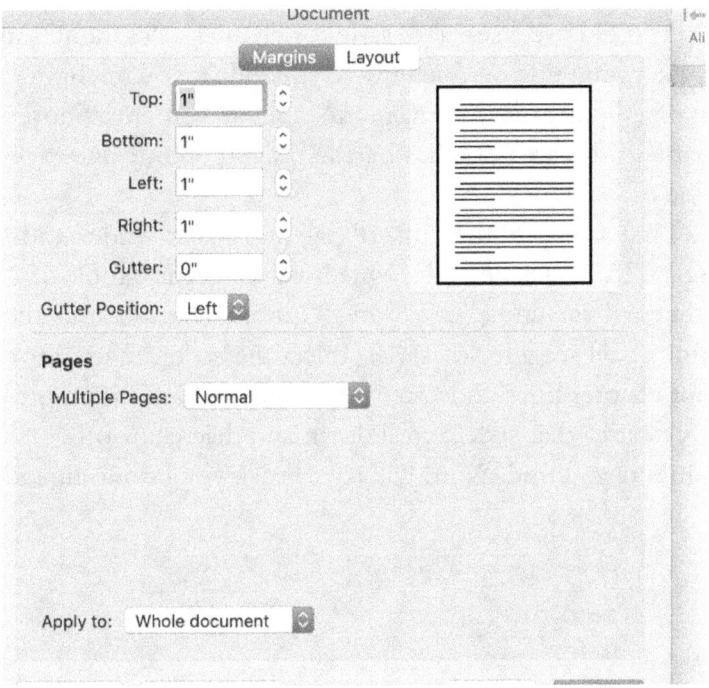

With these tools, you can create a professional-looking book layout, with blank pages where there need to be blank pages, headers and footers where headers and footers belong, and so on.

Table of Contents

A table of contents is important. It is especially helpful when you make a Kindle version with Kindle Create. Here's how.

You did use a separate style for chapter titles, right? And you kept the title on one line. If you didn't, you might do a lot of editing after you make the table of contents. Short chapter titles are good, it's best if they fit on one line in the table of contents.

First, go up to the "Insert" tab and select "Index and Tables." You will get a dialogue box; select the "Table of Contents" tab and click on the "Options" button at the bottom. You'll see a list of styles; select the style you used for your chapter titles and enter the number "1" in the empty box next to that style. Scroll down and delete any other numbers you find. Word will try to trick you into using its

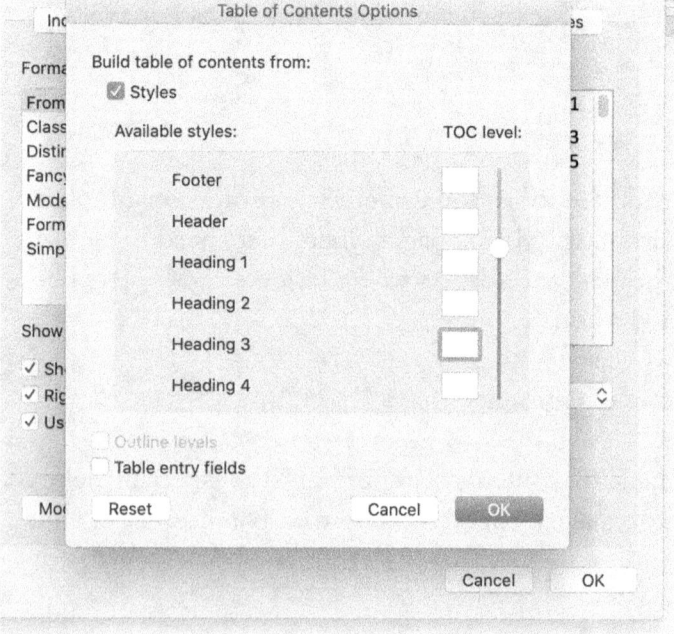

pre-defined headings for your table of contents; don't fall for it.

Back at the second dialogue box, in the "Table of Contents" tab again, you can pick a style for your table of contents. Don't worry; you can change it.

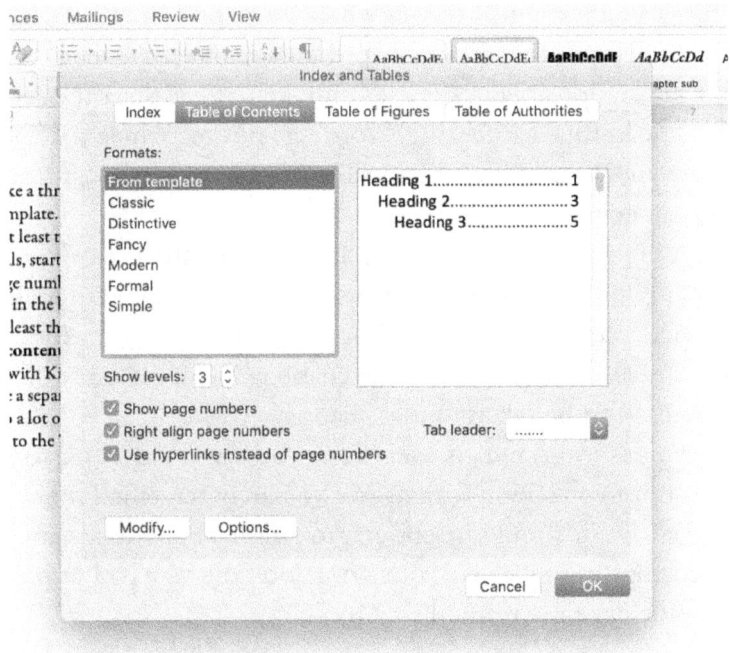

Now go to the page you've set aside for the table of contents, click on it, and like magic, it will insert the table of contents for you. You can edit and change the style of the table of contents just like any other block of text. You will find that right-justified text in the table of contents puts the titles down the left side and the page numbers neatly aligned down the right side, which looks "right."

Moving things around? No worries; you can re-do the table of contents any time. If you end up with double entries because your chapter titles are long, like "Chapter 1" on one line and "And Then the Murders Began" on the next, just edit it until you get what you want. Put "Chapter 1" on the same line as the chapter title manually, delete things you don't want. Or use "shift-return" to start the second line in the chapter title, Word will not recognize that as a new line when it makes the table of contents. It's just text, you can edit it.

A big advantage to making a table of contents in Word is that Kindle Create will start with your Word table to make a hyperlinked table for the e-book. This is huge! It means that the reader can click on the chapter title in the table of contents and be taken to that chapter.

This is by no means everything you can do in Word to customize your book format. We've barely scratched the surface, but it should be enough to amaze your friends and more importantly, make your book look the way you want.

Now it's time to publish. Good luck!

G

Afterword

My intention in offering this book is to share what I have learned about independent publishing as a result of publishing several of my own and others' books through Amazon, Nook, and others. It can be an intimidating process if you don't know what to expect.

This is not the last word on independent publishing, book cover, book design, or Microsoft Word., or anything else, for that matter. Its purpose is to get you started. I know from experience that if you follow these steps you can create a book that you will be proud of. I also know that you will learn much more, including better (for you) ways of doing things.

I hope that this has been helpful. I would like to hear from you if you have comments, suggestions, corrections, or complaints. E-mail me at saminhawaii@hotmail.com with your comments.

And now that you have read this book, you understand why reviews are important, so please, please leave me a review on Amazon.

www.ingramcontent.com/pod-product-compliance
Lightning Source LLC
Chambersburg PA
CBHW070902180526
45168CB00005B/1899

PRAISE FOR TEW

• • •

"The Entrepreneur Within You series makes clear:

If you're waiting for life to get out of the way before starting your business - Fuhgetaboutit! If you do, you will never get started.

Each of the featured entrepreneurs share compelling personal stories. They rise, fall, reflect and rise again. An important read if you want to start a business. Tells you what to expect, avoid and, most importantly, how to achieve success."

Walter M. Perkins, Chicago
Author, Write Right - Right Now - The Book
Available on Amazon.com

###

"TEW takes the fear out of entrepreneurship. After reading this book, you will feel you can conquer any struggle that may come your way. Include this book on your journey!" – Missy B. Salick, Virgo Girl Media, New York, NY

###